An ALCTS Monograph

Linked Data for Cultural Heritage

Edited by
Ed Jones and Michele Seikel

facet
publishing

© American Library Association, 2016

Published by Facet Publishing,
7 Ridgmount Street, London WC1E 7AE
www.facetpublishing.co.uk

Facet Publishing is wholly owned by CILIP: the Chartered Institute
of Library and Information Professionals.

Except as otherwise permitted under the Copyright, Designs and
Patents Act 1988 this publication may only be reproduced, stored or
transmitted in any form or by any means, with the prior permission
of the publisher, or, in the case of reprographic reproduction, in
accordance with the terms of a licence issued by The Copyright
Licensing Agency. Enquiries concerning reproduction outside those
terms should be sent to Facet Publishing, 7 Ridgmount Street,
London WC1E 7AE.

First published in the USA by
the American Library Association, 2016.
This UK edition 2016.

British Library Cataloguing in Publication Data
A catalogue record for this book is available from the British Library.

ISBN 978-1-78330-162-1

Printed and bound in the United Kingdom by Lightning Source.

CONTENTS

INTRODUCTION

Ed Jones

The Web that we experience is designed for people: documents to be read, music, lectures, and so on to be heard; photos, videos, and so on to be viewed; files (spreadsheets, databases, etc.) to be downloaded; and links to be clicked. But of course the Web is also designed for machines, to the extent that machines read the codes and present the results that make it all work.

Over time the Web has evolved some very effective methods for identifying the different parts of a resource using an ever more elaborate hypertext markup language (HTML) and structuring the ways these parts are presented to us visually using cascading style sheets (CSS). The former will tell your browser "this string of text is a main heading" or "this is a bulleted list," while the latter will tell it "main headings should be presented in dark blue bold italic 12-point Times New Roman type" and "bulleted lists appear in dark green 8-point Arial type, with diamonds representing the bullets." And these behind-the-scene methods have become virtually universal on the Web (and much more elaborate than these examples). But introducing semantics to these documents via linked data is like moving from a black-and-white world to a world of color.

Much can be done when machines can process meaning, but that is not possible when the meaning of the documents, and so on, is not understandable by these machines. A machine may know that such-and-such is the main heading in a document, and that this heading is followed by several paragraphs, with images and videos and links to other documents, but that tells the machine nothing about the *meaning* of these things—their *semantics*. What is in the image? Who is the video about? Linked data and its various web standards enable this machine's "understanding" and allow machines to exploit it.

You can see linked data in action today when you perform a Google search for a popular topic. For example, searching for "hunchback of notre dame book" pulls up a web page with the search results on the left and a panel containing various data about the book on the right. The data has been extracted from a variety of online sources and includes star ratings of the book on websites such as Amazon (with links if you want to order a copy), a summary of the book from Wikipedia, a date of first publication, author, characters, links to various sources for reading the book online, and links to other books by Victor Hugo and other books searched for by people who also searched for the *Hunchback of Notre Dame*. If you click on the link to Victor Hugo, that triggers another search and takes you to search results and a panel of similar data on Hugo, with images, a short description, links to his place of birth, death, and burial, and so on. Clicking on his place of birth (Besançon) pulls up yet another collection, this one including a zoomable map of Besançon, its area and population, current weather, current time, and local points of interest. Clicking on the population brings up a chart created from UN data and an invitation to "explore more" by clicking on a small globe symbol. This in turn expands the chart to explore and compare populations for any place(s) in the world. Google calls this the Knowledge Graph, and while the Google Knowledge Graph makes use of some sophisticated data extraction and categorization techniques as well as linked data, it gives you some idea of the potential of linked data as a technique for establishing semantic relationships across the Web.

While this book will be concerned primarily with the use of linked data in the context of so-called cultural heritage institutions—libraries, archives, and museums (LAM)—you can get an idea of the growing scope of the available datasets by examining the list maintained by the World Wide Web Consortium (W3C) at www.w3.org/wiki/TaskForces/CommunityProjects/LinkingOpenData/DataSets.

We are still some distance from the world of linked data that Tim Berners-Lee, James Hendler, and Ora Lassila envisaged fifteen years ago when they first proposed a Semantic Web. In their world, one's mobile device would be able to take a verbal request to make a medical appointment and then automatically negotiate with software at the doctor's office to arrive at the absolutely best of all possible appointments, taking into account (and weighting appropriately) a much larger range of relevant variables than you could ever do on your own.[1] Ideally, from a library's point of view, such a world would also enable devices to automatically select the most appropriate copy of a book, article, and so on for you to read, download, or borrow in a physical form, taking into account your preferred format for delivery, your physical location, the institutions where you have borrowing privileges (and where copies are available), commercial services to which you subscribe, and varying restrictions on access, and so on, that attach to the various available copies. Wouldn't it be lovely?

But such a world represents nirvana. For the time being, we must content ourselves with more modest ambitions for linked open data (LOD). First among these is agreement on standards, for without agreed-upon standards, linking becomes much more problematic and labor-intensive.

FIVE-STAR LINKED OPEN DATA

In 2010 Berners-Lee proposed a five-star scheme for rating linked open data in figure I.1.[2]

It can easily be seen how each additional star makes the data more useful as linked open data. The first star is awarded simply for making the data openly available (even if it's just an image scan of a chart or table, for example). The second star is awarded for giving the data a structure (e.g., spreadsheet or database) that can be read by a program. The third star is awarded for doing so in a nonproprietary format (say, comma-separated values [CSV] for a table).

So far, so easy. The resource usage reports many libraries receive from vendors as part of Project COUNTER would typically be awarded three stars.

But now comes the hard part, where machine-readable structured open data becomes linked open data.

The fourth star is awarded for using open standards from the World Wide Web Consortium (W3C) to give semantic structure to the data, specifically using the resource description framework (RDF) to describe the data and providing a SPARQL endpoint to receive and respond to queries (analogous to a database able to respond to a SQL query). RDF provides a basic structure to

★	Available on the web (whatever format) but with an open license, to be open data
★★	Available as machine-readable structured data (e.g., Excel instead of image scan of a table)
★★★	Same as ★★ but in a non-proprietary format (e.g., CSV instead of Excel)
★★★★	All the above, plus, use open standards from W3C (RDF and SPARQL) to identify things, so that people can point at your stuff
★★★★★	All the above, plus, link your data to other people's data to provide context

Figure I.1 | **Five-star scheme for rating linked open data**

linked data in the form of subject-predicate-object triples (e.g., <thisResource> <hasTitle> <"A la recherché de ma tante perdue">). This basic structure is often elaborated with other vocabularies such as RDFs and OWL (described in more detail in some of our contributions) and various domain-specific vocabularies. For example, the library domain has elaborated various vocabularies for Resource Description and Access (RDA), Functional Requirements of Bibliographic Records (FRBR), and the International Standard Bibliographic Description (ISBD). When your data has achieved four stars, it is in essence "open for business" (though still possibly in want of customers).

Finally, the fifth star is awarded when you take matters into your own hands and begin linking your data to other people's data. At this point, interesting things start happening, like what we experience with those Google Knowledge Graph panels. But creating these links can be very labor-intensive. It's most cost-effective when machines can be called on to do the matching—at least provisionally—as with the virtual international authority file (VIAF), where a commonality of works is used to identify identifiers for the same author in different vocabularies. (For example, it's highly probable that identifier A in vocabulary M represents the same author as identifier B in vocabulary N if both vocabularies identify them as the authors of works X, Y, and Z.)

How many datasets have achieved five stars? A rough idea can be had by periodically viewing the Linked Open Data Cloud at http://lod-cloud.net, which shows datasets clustered in broad categories and linked to one another with varying success (DBpedia and GeoNames are particularly well-connected).

VERY SIMPLE DESCRIPTION OF LINKED DATA

At this point it will be useful to describe, in very broad terms, just what is involved in getting those fourth and fifth stars. A basic understanding of linked data will also help understand the individual contributions to this volume.

In its simplest form, linked data uses the resource description framework and is expressed as three-part statements called triples, each triple consisting of a subject (what the triple is about), a predicate (describing the relationship of the subject to its object), and the object (describing an attribute of the subject or identifying the subject of another triple to which it is related). The subject and predicate are always represented by persistent HTTP URIs (i.e., uniform resource locators [URLs]), where relevant information will be found about them. Ideally, the object is also represented by an HTTP URI, but failing this it may be represented by a literal (such as the transcribed title of a resource). If the object in a triple is represented by an HTTP URI and that HTTP URI is maintained by someone other than you, then you are crossing the border into five-star territory. Congratulations! It is the most difficult border to cross, and many abandon the struggle after a few attempts.

In a given RDF triple, the subject typically represents a resource that you control. For example, subjects in a triplestore representing a library catalog would typically contain HTTP URIs that identify items in the collection (e.g., http://lccn.loc.gov/2013005033).

The predicate, characterizing the relationship between the subject and object, would typically be drawn from a published linked data vocabulary (for example, Schema.org (https://schema.org/docs/schemas.html) or the various vocabularies used for expressing data based on the cataloging standards RDA, FRBR, and ISBD as linked data: www.rdaregistry.info for the RDA vocabularies, http://iflastandards.info/ns/fr/ for the FRBR vocabularies, and http://iflastandards.info/ns/isbd/ for the ISBD vocabularies.

The object may be a literal, especially when it is transcribed data, or it may, like the subject and predicate, be an HTTP URI. This latter case is certainly the preferred one, since linking—that fifth star—becomes problematic without it. The predicate appearing in a triple typically takes a defined value as its object. For example, the predicate RDA carrier type takes values defined at www.rdaregistry.info/termList/RDACarrierType/.

lccn:2013005033 rdam:carrierType rdact:1049

This triple says that the resource identified in the subject (lccn:2013005033), a book called "RDA and Serials Cataloging," has a carrier type (rdam:P3001) of "volume" (rdact:1049). The string of characters (prefix) preceding the colon in each part of the triple is an abbreviated human-readable way of representing the full HTTP URI of the namespace from which the label following the colon is taken. In this case, the subject is taken from the Library of Congress control number namespace, the predicate is taken from the RDA manifestation properties namespace, and the object is taken from the RDA carrier type namespace (a value vocabulary).

While there are only a few legal values for the RDA carrier type, value vocabularies can be quite large. This is especially true in the realm of subject analysis, where an object may be drawn from an extensive vocabulary such as the Library of Congress Subject Headings (http://id.loc.gov/authorities/sub

jects) and legal values can run into the thousands. In such cases, the value can link to the thesaurus, and to triples within that thesaurus that link to related values (for instance, broader or narrower terms), and so on. This is where the power of linked data comes into play.

Let us follow one trail (conceivable but still hypothetical at this point, since the links are not all in place):

lccn:2013005033 rdau:author lccn:n2013018475

lccn:n2013018475 skos:exactMatch viaf:105902737

viaf:105902737 skos:exactMatch isni:000000007525185X

isni:000000007525185X skos:exactMatch orcid:0000000279663733

orcid:0000000279663733 rdau:authorOf doi:10.5860/lrts.54n2.77

These five triples take one from the book (the subject of the first triple) to a journal article by the same author (the object of the fifth triple). The intervening triples take one from the identifier of the author in one identification scheme to the corresponding identifier in another (LC NAF, VIAF, ISNI, and finally ORCID) until one has moved from a scheme designed mainly for library materials (LC NAF) to one designed primarily for scholarly articles, research papers, and so on (ORCID).

SPARQL QUERY LANGUAGE

The preceding set of triples can be traversed iteratively by a human searcher using the linked data query language SPARQL or, preferably, by machine with a rather more complex general-purpose SPARQL query built into the discovery system (for example, your library's discovery system or, perhaps, a web search engine) and hidden from the user, a query that, for example, would routinely retrieve all related materials—whether books or scholarly articles—written by an author whenever one clicked on the author's name in a display of bibliographic data.

Of course, this would require that RDF and other linked data standards be implemented much more broadly than they have been at this point. But the potential of linked data for improving the precision and recall of bibliographic searches should be apparent. The crucial element is linking—that fifth star.

CHALLENGES

Among the challenges to linked open data is the fact that while linked data is increasingly common both on the open web and within enterprises—linked cells in different Excel spreadsheets are a form of internal linked data—and increasing amounts of data, especially government data, are freely available on the open web, combining the two goals—linking and openness—has presented challenges. For example, most ISSN metadata—essential for identifying and linking continuing resources such as scholarly journals—lies behind a paywall, and its sale helps fund the ISSN Network.

But the presence of paywalls and similar barriers does not necessarily preclude the linking of open and proprietary data, though it may restrict the availability of certain linked data to those with the proper credentials.[3]

Beyond this, recent research on RDF triples extracted from nearly 400,000 pay-level domains (PLD) suggests that widespread adoption of both schema .org and linked open data will be dependent on a number of factors, including

- a direct business incentive such as improved listing in search engine results;
- good documentation with ready-to-adapt examples;
- implementation in widely deployed platforms such as Drupal; and
- use of a flexible standard that adapts to widespread violation.[4]

And finally the old bugbear of incorrect data will always be with us: just because metadata is properly structured doesn't mean it's correct. In this regard, I seem to be forever notifying websites—including those using linked data—that I am not the same person as the basketball player Ed "Too Tall" Jones (born the same year as me). I expect that after I'm gone, my descendants will still need to carry on this activity.

So linked open data remains very much a work in progress, and much of the progress has taken place within the domain of the cultural heritage institutions: libraries, archives, and museums. For an accessible and clear-eyed manual for implementing linked data for these institutions, I strongly recommend the excellent book by Seth van Hooland and Ruben Verborgh listed at the end of this chapter.[5] There is no question that the structure of linked data and the machine inferencing it supports shows great promise; many very large datasets have now been made available as RDF, and the SPARQL query language enables sophisticated queries across datasets. The question is, what will be the "killer app" that breaks linked open data out to the wider world and accelerates its uptake? Will it be an incremental extension of schema.org, the linked data vocabulary supported by the major search engines (such as Google and Bing)? Or will there be a thousand flowers blooming and finally achieving a critical mass, as specialized vocabularies enable the optimal exploitation of a variety of domain-specific data sets? Perhaps it will be a project described in this volume.

OUTLINE

In chapter 1, Hilary Thorsen (Stanford University) and M. Cristina Pattuelli (Pratt Institute) survey the use of linked data in significant projects across the cultural heritage domain, including Europeana and the Digital Public Library of America (DPLA), before proceeding to a more detailed description of Linked Jazz, a research project aimed at using linked data technologies "to uncover meaningful connections between documents and data related to the personal and professional lives of jazz artists" and development of related linked data tools and methods.

In chapter 2, Carl Stahmer (University of California, Davis) describes the migration of the renowned English Short Title Catalog (ESTC) from a MARC environment to one of linked data and the possibilities that migration opens up, especially in terms of involving the broader scholarly community in maintaining and enhancing ESTC metadata.

In chapter 3, Allison Jai O'Dell (University of Florida) reviews and reimagines library thesauri, metadata schemas, and information discovery, looking at how controlled vocabularies integrate library practice with linked data and exploring existing practices that are amenable to linked data, as well as areas for expansion of best practices in a linked data environment.

In chapter 4, Iker Huerga (Signifikance) and Michael Lauruhn (Elsevier Labs) examine linked data and authority control from the perspective of STM publishing, describing the role of authority control, identifiers, and vocabularies, including use of the Web Ontology Language (OWL) to add more formal semantics and the use of the SPARQL query language to create mappings between vocabularies.

In chapter 5, Carol Jean Godby (OCLC) describes OCLC's experiments with Schema.org as the foundation for a model of library resource description expressed as linked data, using 900 million catalog records accessible from WorldCat.org.

Godby reports that "OCLC's experiments have shown that Schema.org can be used to define a model . . . which can be expressed in a published standard with institutional backing and potential for widespread adoption."

In chapter 6, Sally McCallum (Library of Congress) relates the development of the Bibliographic Framework Initiative (BIBFRAME) data model, the linked data successor to the data model represented by the MARC 21 formats, describing the fundamental differences between MARC and BIBFRAME. BIBFRAME is designed to be particularly suited as an exchange format for bibliographic data created using Resource Description and Access. The Library of Congress implemented a BIBFRAME pilot in the third quarter of 2015.

As an addendum to the Godby and McCallum contributions (chapters 5 and 6), readers are directed to the executive summary by Godby and Ray Denenberg (Library of Congress) of a technical analysis of the relationship between the LC and OCLC models for library linked data.[6] The technical analysis itself will be released at a later date.

Notes

1. Tim Berners-Lee, James Hendler, and Ora Lassila, "The Semantic Web," *Scientific American* 284, no. 5 (2001): 34–43.
2. Tim Berners-Lee, "Is Your Linked Open Data 5 Star?" in Linked Data, www.w3.org/DesignIssues/LinkedData.html 2010.
3. Carole Jean Goble et al., "Incorporating Commercial and Private Data into an Open Linked Data Platform for Drug Discovery," *Lecture Notes in Computer Science* 8219 (2013): 65–80. doi: 10.1007/978–3–642–41338–4_5.
4. Heiko Paulheim, "What the Adoption of schema.org Tells about Linked Open Data," *JCEUR Workshop Proceedings* 1362 (2015): 84–90. http://ceur-ws.org/Vol-1362/PROFILES2015_paper6.pdf.
5. Seth van Hooland and Ruben Verborgh, *Linked Data for Libraries, Archives and Museums: How to Clean, Link and Publish Your Metadata* (Chicago: Neal-Schuman, 2014).
6. Carol Jean Godby and Ray Denenberg, *Common Ground: Exploring Compatibilities between the Linked Data Models of the Library of Congress and OCLC* (Dublin, Ohio: Library of Congress and OCLC Research, 2015), www.oclc.org/content/dam/research/publications/2015/oclcresearch-loc-linked-data-2015-a4.pdf.

Further Reading

Allemang, Dean, and Jim Hendler. *Semantic Web for the Working Ontologist.* Amsterdam: Morgan Kaufmann, 2011.

Antoniou, Grigoris, and Frank van Harmelen. *A Semantic Web Primer.* 3rd ed. Cambridge, Mass.: MIT Press, 2012.

Breitman, Karin K., Marco Antonio Casanova, and Walter Truszkowski. *Semantic Web: Concepts, Technologies and Applications.* London: Springer, 2007. doi: 10.1007/978-1 –84628–710–7.

Coyle, Karen. *Linked Data Tools: Connecting on the Web.* Chicago: American Library Association, 2012. doi: 10.5860/ltr.48n4.

Godby, Carol Jean, Shenghui Wang, and Jeffrey K. Mixter. *Library Linked Data in the Cloud: OCLC's Experiments with New Models of Resources Description.* San Rafael, CA: Morgan & Claypool Publishers, 2015. doi: 10.2200/S00620ED1V01Y201412WBE012.

Heath, Tom, and Christian Bizer. *Linked Data: Evolving the Web into a Global Data Space.* San Rafael, CA: Morgan & Claypool Publishers, 2011. doi: 10.2200/S00334ED1V01Y201102WBE001.

Wood, David, Marsha Zaidman, and Luke Ruth. *Linked Data: Structured Data on the Web.* Shelter Island, NY: Manning, 2014.

LINKED OPEN DATA AND THE CULTURAL HERITAGE LANDSCAPE

Hilary K. Thorsen and M. Cristina Pattuelli

Linked open data is assuming an increasingly central role in how cultural institutions organize and share their data on the Web. The open and unified information environment that the LOD initiative is actively building has enormous potential for addressing some of the enduring issues in the field of cultural heritage, including data interoperability and integration. The "walled gardens" approach to data management in libraries, archives, and museums, as well as other cultural organizations, often has the unintended consequence of limiting access to and use of cultural heritage materials. LOD, on the other hand, with its principle of openness, offers an opportunity to expose data currently siloed in databases or institutional repositories and foster greater collaboration among cultural institutions across domains. Creating this expanded, even boundless scenario requires a radical revision of our approach to traditional data representation, curation, and discovery.

Libraries, museums, and archives have historically developed diverse and often divergent descriptive practices that are tailored to local forms of access and use of resources rooted in the analog world. The new representational and technological framework that linked data provides offers a unifying methodology for creating, sharing, and reusing data and metadata across domains. This model makes it possible for different communities to collaborate without the need for coordination, because the sharing of common representational conventions no longer requires a priori agreements on schemas. For example, vocabularies from different domains, when expressed in RDF, can be recombined and expanded through the mixing and matching of terms. In the broadest sense, LOD brings to libraries, archives, and museums a new way of thinking about the information object and its boundaries centered on entities and their relationships rather than documents. This makes it possible for atomic bits of content to be interlinked from heterogeneous sources, from the humanities to the sciences, in unprecedented ways, creating new and meaningful pathways to discovery and navigation.

Digital cultural heritage is becoming an integral part of an extended and expanded web of data through the work of Linked Open Data in Libraries, Archives, and Museums (LODLAM).[1] LODLAM, an international community of information professionals, researchers, and educators, is actively working to promote the convergence of cultural heritage communities through the implementation of linked open data principles and technology. Emerging in 2011, LODLAM has progressed from a small grassroots effort to a growing movement at the forefront of sowing the culture of linked data in cultural heritage communities through LOD research and implementation. The LODLAM community has expanded and evolved through a series of initiatives and events, from biannual international summits to regional meetings that bring together people from different cultural contexts and organizations to share case studies, experience, and ideas to advance LOD development in cultural heritage.

While we have only begun to envision the potential for cultural organizations to permeate the Web with open cultural heritage data, considerable efforts are being made towards devising appropriate practices and building effective applications needed to create and consume cultural LOD. The LOD landscape for cultural heritage is now not only extensive, but also highly diversified. Led by some of the world's most important national libraries, including the British Library, the Bibliothèque Nationale de France, and the Deutsche National Bibliothek, libraries have paved the way by contributing their legacy data to the LOD ecosystem and making the LOD pool of data grow exponentially. To provide an overview of the range of LOD activities and to illustrate some of the challenges and opportunities LOD presents for the cultural heritage community, we have identified a representative sample of projects from the arts and humanities, ranging from large-scale resource aggregators to smaller experimental initiatives.

EUROPEANA

Perhaps the best-known linked data cultural heritage project is Europeana, an online platform launched in 2008 that aggregates cultural heritage data from 2,300 small and large libraries, archives, and museums in Europe.[2] Currently it contains descriptions and thumbnails for more than 33 million cultural objects that link to the source objects on the institutions' websites. With a single access point to cultural heritage data, users are not constrained by typical institutional silos, enabling them to search and browse across institutions, collections, formats, and countries situating these objects within a broader cultural context. As an open and authoritative source of cultural heritage data, Europeana began publishing a pilot subset of its data as LOD in 2011 and currently has 20 million cultural objects in its dataset.[3]

Implementing LOD at Europeana required overcoming a number of obstacles. One of the most difficult challenges was the mental shift required of cultural heritage institutions forced to consider how their collections integrate with and contribute to a wider information continuum.[4] Since openness of the data is key to Europeana's linked data vision, they needed to convince cultural heritage institutions to release their data. Their approach was to launch a highly successful online video campaign demonstrating how releasing data benefits users and generates interest among new users as the data is reused in novel ways. Since 2012, the open data released has grown from 2.4 million to 20 million objects.

Europeana has also had to deal with the extremely heterogeneous data from its 2,300 providers, which is described according to a wide variety of formats ranging from international standards to homegrown schemas.[5] The Europeana Data Model (EDM) was developed to make them interoperable. The EDM allows complex, hierarchically structured objects and entities to be represented while attaching provenance to each resource. It successfully reuses and links to existing vocabularies, such as Dublin Core and SKOS, but has run into problems with provenance and licensing information, critical for users of cultural items and their providers. To associate provenance information with each object, Europeana combined a number of existing means to supply this necessary information as it waits for working groups to adopt a standard approach.

To stimulate and support reuse of its data, Europeana devotes a section of its website to professionals so librarians, archivists, and curators can exchange information, share their projects, and connect. A special Labs portal serves as a place of experimentation for developers to access Europeana's data through its application profile interface (API) and share their work. Serendip-o-matic, which helps users discover sources within Europeana and other cultural portals related to their research interests, and Storyana, which develops stories using Wikipedia articles and Europeana content, are just two examples of the kind of innovation Europeana's open approach has spawned.

DIGITAL PUBLIC LIBRARY OF AMERICA

The U.S. counterpart to Europeana is the Digital Public Library of America (DPLA).[6] The DPLA collects millions of resources from America's libraries, archives, and museums and makes them available through a single access point. The goal of the DPLA is to ensure all types of materials ranging from written text and artwork to scientific datasets and oral histories are freely available, discoverable, and usable. To accomplish this goal, DPLA delivers content through an online portal that can be searched and browsed in a variety of ways. It includes an interactive time line and map as well as a virtual bookshelf. Similar to Europeana, DPLA publishes its data through an API in J-SON-LD, a linked data serialization, so that the data can be used for new purposes, including apps.

DPLA prioritizes demonstrations of what can be done with its openly available linked data dataset. The general public can submit ideas for DPLA apps and tools, which are shared with the community. People can declare that they will work on something themselves or request someone else to develop it, making it easy for developers, programmers, and engineers to know what DPLA users would find most useful for their research. Once apps have been designed that use DPLA data or tools created that assist others in more easily making use of DPLA's data, they are showcased in the App Library.[7]

SOCIAL NETWORKS AND ARCHIVAL CONTEXT PROJECT

Based in the archival community, the Social Networks and Archival Context (SNAC) Project intends to create software and LOD resources to make connections between people and archival descriptions, authority files, and library catalogs.[8] Archival description has traditionally been restricted intellectually and functionally by mixing record and context descriptions. It is the aim of SNAC to facilitate archival research for users by improving their searches for people, families, and organizations and their understanding of the socio-historical context in which documents are situated by exposing the social connections between people and historical records. Archivists will further benefit with an increase in efficiency through the reuse of resource description.[9]

Data for SNAC is extracted from archival source descriptions and used to create records for persons, families, and organizations using the Encoded Archival Context-Corporate Bodies, Persons, and Families (EAC-CPF) standard. In the prototype SNAC interface, users can browse or search for records that contain the preferred form of name, alternate forms of name, occupations, topical subject headings, biographical entries, and links to archival collections and resources created by or related to the entity and other related named entities, which are used to construct a social network.[10] SNAC had 3.7 million entities from 4,000 repositories as of 2015.

SNAC faced significant challenges with identities, as multiple data sources made it possible for multiple URIs and records to be created for the same entity.[11] Given the vast number of records, the reconciliation of these names was and is a time-consuming and daunting process. Improvement in the quality of results has been further complicated by the heterogeneous nature of the archival descriptions, but it is hoped that future research and development will identify new automated solutions. In response, a national archival authorities program cooperative that describes and enhances authorities and manages and disambiguates identities is in development.[12]

REGESTA.EXE

The Italian company, regesta.exe, works on projects to improve the technologies used to make digital content available on the Web. They recently began experimenting with linked data on a couple of archival projects. The Repository for Linked Open Archival Data (RELOAD) project explores the methodology needed to expose archival resources from various archival collections as linked data.[13] Using data from the Istituto dei Beni Culturali Regione Emilia Romagna and Archivio Centrale della Stato, it plans to become a central repository for archival descriptions that can be easily accessed and shared. In order to transform archival descriptions into linked data and to model classes and properties of archival data, it created an ontology, Ontology of Archival Description (OAD), using the Web Ontology Language (OWL). OAD was used to transform Encoded Archival Description (EAD) files to RDF/XML files using an XSL stylesheet. For records of people, corporate bodies, and families, the EAC-CPF Ontology was used to transform the EAC-CPF records to linked data.[14] The archival descriptions can be searched, browsed via facets, or viewed in graph form.

A second archival project involves the records of the Contemporary Jewish Documentation Center Foundation (CDEC). It holds the largest collection of Holocaust documents in Italy. Regesta.exe is working to create a digital library with LOD as the information structure.[15] As part of this goal, the Shoah Ontology was created to link CDEC's database of 8,000 names of Jewish victims of the Holocaust in Italy with resources and names in other archives and linked open datasets.[16] The ontology relates the "persecution" class, which describes arrest, imprisonment, and deportation, and the "person" class, which contains the biographical information of the victims. While the ontology describes the persecution and deportation of Jews in Italy between 1943 and 1945, it is hoped that it will eventually expand to represent the Shoah as a whole.

AMSTERDAM MUSEUM

Museum data has traditionally been the least exposed of cultural heritage data. Licensing and provenance information are extremely important for museums for maintaining their credibility and trustworthiness within the art world, so museum data must be perfect before it can be published online. However, more recently, museums have begun to experiment with LOD to expose their data as a means of increasing the visibility of their collections on the Web. The Amsterdam Museum was an early adopter of LOD. Because of physical limitations, it is only possible to display 20 percent of the museum's collection at any given time, so in 2010 the museum made its collection available online under a Creative Commons license.[17] The collection can be browsed online, with its metadata retrievable through an API. Utilizing the Europeana Data

Model, the data has been converted into a five-star Linked Data set, which means the HTTP URIs in the dataset provide useful information and link to other URIs to enable further discovery.

Often when an institution's data is mapped to a standard that increases its interoperability, it loses some of the richness and detail that may have been present in the original. Fortunately, the museum did not lose this robust descriptive content because the museum's thesaurus of 28,000 concepts and person authority file with almost 67,000 persons in addition to the over 70,000 object descriptions were converted to preserve internal links within the dataset.[18] Links to external datasets included GeoNames for geographical concepts, the Dutch Art and Architecture thesaurus for non-geographical concepts, and the Getty Union List of Artist Names (ULAN) for people. The museum's LOD dataset is available through Europeana and will serve as a model within Europeana for future metadata conversions.

SMITHSONIAN MUSEUM OF AMERICAN ART

More recently, the Smithsonian Museum of American Art converted its dataset of 41,000 objects and 8,000 artists to linked data.[19] Because much of the data museums collect and retain must remain private, especially donor and financial information, publishing the data openly can be difficult. For this project, the Smithsonian converted only the data for the collection that is already published on the website. Because of its complicated and rich hierarchical metadata, choosing the ontologies for mapping the data was especially challenging. Ultimately, the museum selected the Dublin Core, FOAF, SKOS, RDA Group Elements, schema.org, and EDM ontologies for mapping their data. Data was then linked to external sources, including DBPedia for artist biographies, the *New York Times* for obituaries, exhibition and publication reviews, and auction results, as well as the Getty ULAN identifiers.[20]

As a result of the process, the museum developed tools that anyone can use to convert their data to linked data. One is Karma, which uses an automated process to integrate data from various sources based on an ontology and publish it in RDF.[21] Data can then be linked externally with a high level of accuracy and experts can review and curate links to ensure the data meets the high standards that museums require. With its LOD, the museum intends to continue developing new applications, including a virtual museum where works held at various museums are brought together as well as a tool to create multimedia stories about art. The museum will also lead the American Art Collaborative, a consortium of fourteen American museums that will use LOD to bring greater access, research and scholarship, and collaboration to American art.[22]

LINKED JAZZ

Similar to other cultural heritage projects, the authors' project, Linked Jazz, has evolved in an experimental way and through an iterative process, facing some of the challenges common to this pioneering phase of LOD development. For this reason, Linked Jazz provides a representative case study grounded in a real-world application scenario. Given the familiarity with the project, we will provide an extensive overview of Linked Jazz, highlighting its various components and phases of development to share outcomes as well as lessons learned.

Linked Jazz is an ongoing project based at Pratt Institute's School of Information and Library Science that explores the application of LOD principles and technology to digital cultural heritage materials with the goal of enhancing their discovery, visibility, and ultimately interpretation and use.[23] Started in 2011 thanks to an OCLC/ALISE Research Grant, the project has focused on using oral histories from digital archives of jazz history to provide jazz researchers, educators, and the general public with new ways to discover and engage with archival content.

The immediate goal of the project was to leverage LOD technology to represent and visualize the complex network of relationships held among jazz musicians as described in oral histories. The unprecedented availability of digitized text offers researchers a unique opportunity to conduct network analysis on a large scale. Using LOD technology to represent network data from primary sources is a novel approach that offers remarkable advantages to researchers, including making this data machine-processable and freely available and reusable in various contexts and for different applications and data services. The set of network data can then be interlinked with external sources that exist in the open linked data cloud so that new associations between data and between resources can be identified. Applying LOD to archival documents and special collections makes information that is otherwise contained, if not hidden, in primary sources and typically scattered across collections and institutions more easily available. Researchers can access and navigate this content in a unified and integrated way that is useful for enhancing discovery and facilitating analysis. Even though the Web has made archival content more accessible, the research process required for locating resources and collecting data continues to often be hard and labor-intensive. For example, the task of identifying and presenting the relationships that exist within a social group such as the jazz community as a cohesive set of data would require digging into several digital libraries and archives and sifting through documents that even experienced researchers can find difficult to locate.

This approach, however, required the development of a whole array of methods and tools needed to create linked data from textual resources and to expose and visualize it. The project has progressed in an iterative way through a number of phases including

1. the creation of RDF triples from textual documents;
2. the curation of data to ensure data quality;
3. the visualization of the dataset; and
4. the semantic enrichment of the data.

While most of the current LOD projects in the cultural heritage domain are concerned with converting legacy metadata into RDF triples (for instance, cultural heritage data aggregators Europeana and DPLA as well as single-institution projects including the Smithsonian Museum of American Art), Linked Jazz focuses on the content of the document as the source of linked data rather than its description. The possibility to leverage unstructured textual data, in addition to bibliographic metadata, can augment the reach of LOD technology exponentially. It requires, however, a different development process and a suitable set of tools.

The first step was to perform the extraction of proper names of musicians from interview transcripts and associate these names in order to create a social network. The underlying assumption behind this method is such that if the subject of an interview mentions an individual, we can infer that some type of connection, even a very basic familiarity, should exist with that person. To process oral histories, the *Transcript Analyzer* was developed to perform named entity recognition (NER) to locate instances of personal names in text. More specifically, this tool extracts proper names and identifies basic relationships between people based on their mention in the text. See figure 1.1.[24]

To detect proper names the Transcript Analyzer relies on a directory of jazz musician names that serves to support the matching of the name instances. Such a domain-specific name vocabulary had to be created from scratch and was derived from DBpedia. While the details of its creation are described elsewhere,

Figure 1.1 | **The Transcript Analyzer tool**

it is worthwhile to mention the need to address issues of data quality, as is often the case when dealing with large user-generated datasets.[25] While DBpedia is a rich source of linked data resulting from the extraction of structured data from Wikipedia, the data also contains a good deal of noise. Proper names of artists, with their array of aliases and stage names, are particularly prone to inconsistency and ambiguity, including homonyms, different spellings, and misspellings. For example, *Duke Ellington* presents six alternate names including spelling variants and nicknames—*Ellington, Edward Kennedy; Ellington, Diuk; Turner, Joe; Greer, Sonny; Duke, Obie; and Ellington, Obie Duke*—as per the Library of Congress name authority record.[26]

Curatorial work is an essential component in LOD development that is required to address various issues of data quality.[27] To make our jazz name vocabulary as inclusive and accurate as possible, we mapped individuals' URIs onto the Library of Congress Name Authority File and Virtual International Authority File (VIAF) to disambiguate and enrich the data with name variants from authority records. Figure 1.2 gives an integrated view of Duke Ellington's preferred and alternate names included in the Linked Jazz name directory.

The mapping process was supported by a dedicated application, now in the process of being redesigned, that delivered results grouped by degrees of confidence.[28] See figure 1.3. A perfect match is counted when both name strings and corresponding birth and death dates overlap. Results with a lower level of confidence can then be manually revised to disambiguate homonyms as well as to validate or remove uncertain matches.

Preferred Name	<skos:prefLabel>	Ellington, Duke, 1899-1974
Alternate Name	<skos:altLabel>	Ellington, Edward Kennedy, 1899-1974
Alternate Name	<skos:altLabel>	Ellington, Diuk, 1899-1974
Alternate Name	<skos:altLabel>	Turner, Joe, 1899-1974
Alternate Name	<skos:altLabel>	Greer, Sonny, 1899-1974
Alternate Name	<skos:altLabel>	Ellington, Obie Duke, 1889-1974
Alternate Name	<skos:altLabel>	Duke, Obie, 1889-1974

Figure 1.2 | **Duke Ellington's preferred and alternate names included in the Linked Jazz name directory**

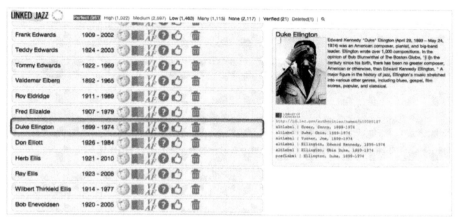

Figure 1.3 | **The name mapping and curation tool**

More than fifty digitized interview transcripts from special collections and jazz archives in the United States have now been processed through the Transcript Analyzer resulting in a dataset of approximately 15,000 RDF triples.[29] Each triple represents a connection between musicians expressed through the predicate rel:knowsOf, shown here:

<http://linkedjazz.org/resource/Stanley_Kay>
<http://purl.org/vocab/relationship/knowsOf>
<http://linkedjazz.org/resource/Duke_Ellington>.

It is often noted that the benefits of linked data cannot be conveyed in a vacuum. As an effective way to make the Linked Jazz data easily accessible and

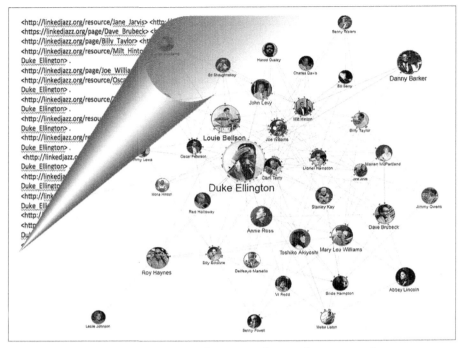

Figure 1.4 | **The RDF triples power the network visualization tool to reveal Duke Ellington's social network**

usable, we developed a visualization tool that displays the web of relationships existing in our dataset.[30] See figure 1.4. The nodes in the network represent jazz artists and the edges denote their relations. Nodes and edges are labeled with a Unique Resource Identifier (URI) as the application is driven by our linked open dataset. Figure 1.5 provides a sample of RDF triples representing the relationships between musicians at the back end of the network visualization tool.

This is a highly interactive tool that allows users to explore and analyze the network through different views. For example, users can navigate the network dynamically by drilling down to a musician's personal circles or ego-network. Each musician-node is associated with their biographical sketch derived from Wikipedia and even a sample of their work through an audio clip. Individuals can also be clustered into subgroups based on the relationships they share, or selected from a list to verify whether a connection between them exists and reveal other shared connections. See figure 1.6. Another distinctive feature of the tool is the possibility to easily and directly review the source of the connection

<http://linkedjazz.org/resource/Jane_Jarvis><http://purl.org/vocab/relationship/ knowsOf><http://linkedjazz.org/resource/Duke_Ellington>.

<https://linkedjazz.org/page/Dave_Brubeck><http://purl.org/vocab/relationship/ knowsOf><http://linkedjazz.org/resource/Duke_Ellington>.

<http://linkedjazz.org/page/Billy_Taylor><http://purl.org/vocab/relationship/ knowsOf><http://linkedjazz.org/resource/Duke_Ellington>.

<http://linkedjazz.org/resource/Milt_Hinton><http://purl.org/vocab/relationship/ knowsOf><http://linkedjazz.org/resource/Duke_Ellington>.

<http://linkedjazz.org/page/Joe_Williams><http://purl.org/vocab/relationship/ knowsOf><http://linkedjazz.org/resource/Duke_Ellington>.

<http://linkedjazz.org/resource/Oscar_Peterson><http://purl.org/vocab/ relationship/knowsOf><http://linkedjazz.org/resource/Duke_Ellington>.

Figure 1.5 | **Sample of RDF triples that drive the network visualization tool**

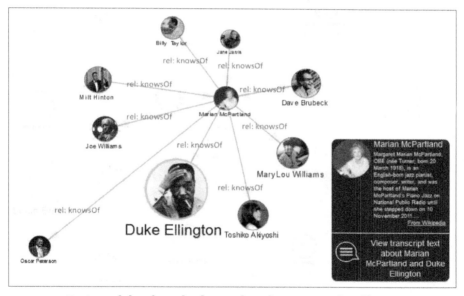

Figure 1.6 | **A view of the shared relationships between Duke Ellington and Marian McPartland**

by mousing-over an edge. The interview passage that mentions the relationship pops up providing context to the data and provenance.

The Linked Jazz network reveals how the jazz community is highly inter-connected. As our dataset continues to grow, the size and accuracy of the social network will also increase, supporting more comprehensive analyses of its structure and dynamics. To dig deeper into the nuanced nature of the human relationships expressed by a social network, a whole new set of methods and tools are needed to be able to determine the specific meaning of these relationships and assign them granular semantics.

Traditional natural language processing (NLP) methods, such as the ones employed in our Transcript Analyzer, are of limited help for identifying the semantics of human relationships with its degree of granularity and nuances. In general, performing complex semantic analysis of text through automated methods is computationally extremely arduous. To classify the relationships detected with the Transcript Analyzer, our automated approach was complemented by a human-driven one based on crowd-sourcing. To this end, we developed a tool, *Linked Jazz 52nd Street*, which engages jazz experts and enthusiasts with helping to interpret the relationships in the transcripts.[31] This is a web-based application that asks contributors to label the relationships between two jazz musicians by choosing from a list of options. See figure 1.7. The pool of possible relationships is derived from well-established RDF vocabularies and the user's selection is automatically converted into an RDF triple.

To compile the list of relationships, suitable RDF vocabularies were identified including the Relationship vocabulary, FOAF, and the Music Ontology.[32] Candidate relationships were selected by analyzing and mapping person-related predicates (Pattuelli, 2011).[33] The final set covers lower degrees of personal closeness (e.g., knows_of, has_met) as well as deeper levels of social

Figure 1.7 | **The Linked Jazz 52nd Street classifier interface**

and professional ties (e.g., collaborated_with, influenced_by, and mentor_of). Aligning vocabulary terms helps to ensure that terms in existing vocabularies are reused where applicable and that new terms are consistently integrated with the existing ones. Jazz experts were also consulted to determine which of these relationships would be most appropriate and useful to them and the broader community of users of jazz archives.

Linked Jazz 52nd Street participants are presented with segments of the interview transcript where a musician is mentioned and are prompted to choose the most suitable label, as discussed earlier. The output of these tasks is in the form of RDF triples that feed back into the project's set of linked data and thus will semantically enhance the social network. See figures 1.8 and 1.9.

In addition to supporting a sophisticated data service specific to the project, this tool has the potential to engage the community of jazz researchers and enthusiasts as well as the general public with primary sources and archival collections, increasing their visibility and use. Designing crowd-sourcing tools is challenging, because many complex elements need to be considered to make the system successful and sustainable. For example, different types of motivational factors are at the root of active and continued engagement by contributors.[34]

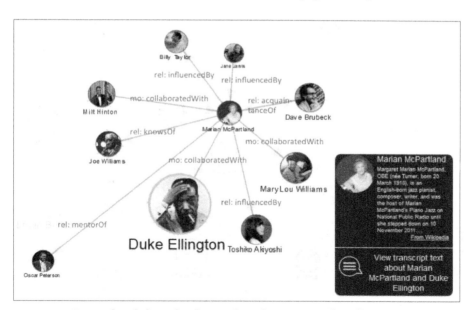

Figure 1.8 | **Example of shared relationships between Duke Ellington and Marian McPartland semantically enhanced via crowd-sourcing**

<http://linkedjazz.org/resource/Marian_McPartland><http://purl.org/vocab/relationship/influencedBy><http://linkedjazz.org/resource/Jane_Jarvis>.

<http://linkedjazz.org/resource/Marian_McPartland><http://purl.org/vocab/relationship/acquaintanceOf><https://linkedjazz.org/resource/Dave_Brubeck>.

<http://linkedjazz.org/resource/Marian_McPartland><http://purl.org/vocab/relationship/influencedBy><http://linkedjazz.org/resource/Billy_Taylor>.

<http://linkedjazz.org/resource/Marian_McPartland><http://purl.org/ontology/mo/collaborated_with><http://linkedjazz.org/resource/Milt_Hinton>.

<http://linkedjazz.org/resource/Marian_McPartland><http://purl.org/vocab/relationship/knowsOf><http://linkedjazz.org/resource/Joe_Williams>.

<http://linkedjazz.org/resource/Marian_McPartland><http://purl.org/vocab/relationship/mentorOf><http://linkedjazz.org/resource/Oscar_Peterson>.

<http://linkedjazz.org/resource/Marian_McPartland><http://purl.org/ontology/mo/collaborated_with><http://linkedjazz.org/resource/Duke_Ellington>.

<http://linkedjazz.org/resource/Marian_McPartland><http://purl.org/vocab/relationship/influencedBy><http://linkedjazz.org/resource/Toshiko_Akiyoshi>.

<http://linkedjazz.org/resource/Marian_McPartland><http://purl.org/ontology/mo/collaborated_with><http://linkedjazz.org/resource/Mary_Lou_Williams>.

<http://linkedjazz.org/resource/Jane_Jarvis><http://purl.org/vocab/relationship/knowsOf><http://linkedjazz.org/resource/Duke_Ellington>.

<https://linkedjazz.org/page/Dave_Brubeck><http://purl.org/vocab/relationship/mentorOf><http://linkedjazz.org/resource/Duke_Ellington>.

<http://linkedjazz.org/page/Billy_Taylor><http://purl.org/vocab/relationship/knowsOf><http://linkedjazz.org/resource/Duke_Ellington>.

<http://linkedjazz.org/resource/Milt_Hinton><http://purl.org/vocab/relationship/knowsOf><http://linkedjazz.org/resource/Duke_Ellington>.

<http://linkedjazz.org/page/Joe_Williams><http://purl.org/vocab/relationship/knowsOf><http://linkedjazz.org/resource/Duke_Ellington>.

<http://linkedjazz.org/resource/Oscar_Peterson><http://purl.org/vocab/relationship/mentorOf><http://linkedjazz.org/resource/Duke_Ellington>.

<http://linkedjazz.org/resource/Toshiko_Akiyoshi><http://purl.org/vocab/relationship/knowsOf><http://linkedjazz.org/resource/Duke_Ellington>.

<http://linkedjazz.org/resource/Mary_Lou_Williams><http://purl.org/ontology/mo/collaborated_with><http://linkedjazz.org/resource/Duke_Ellington>.

Figure 1.9 | **RDF triples of the shared relationships between Duke Ellington and Marian McPartland**

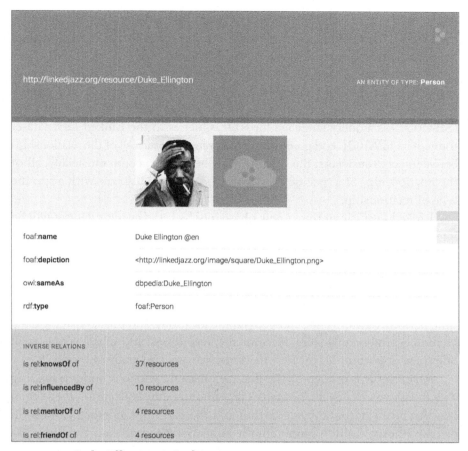

Figure 1.10 | **Duke Ellington's LodView page**

A number of features were included in the design of Linked Jazz 52nd Street in order to maximize crowd participation over time. A dynamic ego network and a progress bar were among the features introduced to provide immediate visual feedback on the user's progress with the intent of making their work recognizable and transparent. New iterations of testing and refinements are planned to further the development of this tool. As of today, Linked Jazz 52nd Street has been used by approximately 500 registered users and has resulted in the classification of more than 15,000 relationships.

The Linked Jazz resources, essentially person entities and their predicates, can also be viewed with LodView, an open-source publishing platform for LOD datasets.[35] See figure 1.10. LodView displays LOD resources as web pages, in line with one of the key principles of linked data that requires that each URI is "dereferenceable," meaning that it resolves to a web page that can be looked up by humans and machines.

In line with Linked Open Data's principles of data sharing and reuse and best practices, the Linked Jazz dataset is accessible via an API, as well as a SPARQL endpoint.[36] SPARQL Protocol and RDF Query Language (SPARQL) is a query language for RDF. Queries to the Linked Jazz dataset through its SPARQL end point would, for example, return all of the relationships between jazz musicians, the relationships between specific musicians, all of the relationships of a specific musician, or all of the musicians with a specific type of relationship.

Linked Jazz is entering a new phase in which the current dataset will be interlinked with external LOD sources to further increase its richness. Mashups with triples representing discographies, musician photographs, performances, and library holdings will expand traditional access to archival content with the ultimate goal of making it part of a global and integrated discovery environment. Bringing together a broad range of spatial and temporal data, including time periods, dates, events, and geographic locations, and music-specific data, including professional roles, instruments, recordings, and music venues, will offer new opportunities for information discovery and analysis.

An example is offered by the first data mashup which is under way using data from two of Tulane University's jazz photography collections, the Hogan Jazz Archive Photography collection and the Ralston Crawford Collection of Jazz Photography. Combined, the collections contain more than 1,700 images in which more than 2,700 individuals are depicted, 681 being unique individuals. Based on the assumption that people depicted in the same photo are likely to know each other, triples are created that express exactly this type of relationship through the predicate foaf:knows.

In this instance, our source of data was the metadata describing the photographs. As is to be expected with most cultural heritage resources, Tulane's metadata did not come in the form of linked data and thus it needed to be converted into LOD. The process consisted of cleaning and normalizing the data, including mapping the proper names of the musicians depicted to name authorities. As an example of how the process works, one of the photographs in the Hogan Jazz Archive's Collection depicts Duke Ellington and Louie Armstrong at a party held in their honor along with other guests in Chicago on February 14, 1935. In the original metadata record, specifically in the subject field, their names appear as Ellington, Duke and Armstrong, Louis, 1901–1971.

By matching these names to DBpedia, triples were created that, for example, would describe Ellington as a foaf:person with a foaf:name associated with it. Ellington was then linked to the photograph using the predicate foaf:depiction and to Armstrong using foaf:knows. Finally, the date and the place the photograph was taken in were also linked to the photograph using the predicates dc:created and dc:spatial. Figure 1.11 shows the triple structure in the left column and instances from the specific example concerning Ellington and Armstrong in the right.

As the phase of data conversion and triple creation is concluded, the next step will be to integrate the Tulane data with the existing dataset and enhance

<personURI> <http://www.w3.org/1999/02/ 22-rdf-syntax-ns#type> <http://xmlns.com/foaf/0.1/ Person>.	<http://dbpedia.org/resource/Duke_Ellington> <http://www.w3.org/1999/02/22-rdf-syntax-ns #type> <http://xmlns.com/foaf/0.1/Person>.
<personURI> <http://xmlns.comfoaf/0.1/name> "First Last"@en.	<http://dbpedia.org/resource/Duke_Ellington> <http://xmlns.com/foaf/0.1/name> "Duke Ellington"@en.
<personURI> <http://xmlns.com/foaf/0.1/ depiction> <photoURI>.	<http://dbpedia.org/resource/Duke_Ellington> <http://xmlns.com/foaf/0.1/depiction> <http://louisdl.louislibraries.org/cdm/singleitem/ collection/p16313coll33/id/1689/rec/1>.
<person1URI> <http://xmlns.com/foaf/0.1/knows> <person2URI>.	<http://dbpedia.org/resource/Duke_Ellington> <http://xmlns.com/foaf/0.1/knows> <http://dbpedia.org/resource/Louie_Armstrong>.
<photoURI> <http://purl.org/dc/terms/created> "YYYY-MM-DD"^^<http://www .w3.org/2001/XMLSchema #date>.	<http://louisdl.louislibraries.org/cdm/singleitem/ collection/p16313coll33/id/1689/rec/1> <http://purl.org/dc/terms/created> "1935-02-14"^^<http://www.w3.org/2001/XML Schema#date>.
<photoURI> <http://purl.org/dc/terms/spatial> <geonamesURI>.	<http://louisdl.louislibraries.org/cdm/singleitem/ collection/p16313coll33/id/1689/rec/1> <http://purl.org/dc/terms/spatial> <http://www.geonames.org/4887398/chicago. html>.

Figure 1.11 | **RDF triples representing Duke Ellington and Louis Armstrong**

the Linked Jazz dataset with links to the actual photographs and their source archives.[37]

The suite of tools developed for Linked Jazz is freely available on GitHub.[38] Following prototyping development methodology, these tools will continue to be improved through iterations of testing. Plans are under way to continue the development of the chain of tools to reach their full implementation. The goal is to increase their versatility so that they can be applied to different contexts of use and maximize their usability, considering librarians and archivists as the primary users. Lessons learned are shared through documentation intended to contribute to establishing best practices in LOD development for libraries, archives, and museums.

Notes

1. "LODLAM: Linked Open Data in Libraries, Archives, and Museums," http://lodlam.net.
2. Europeana, http://europeana.eu.
3. "Europeana Linked Open Data," Europeana Labs, http://labs.europeana.eu/api/linked -open-data/introduction/.
4. Cesare Concordia, Stefan Gradmann, and Siberd Siebinga, "Not Just Another Portal, Not Just Another Digital Library: A Portrait of Europeana as an Application Program Interface," *IFLA Journal* 36 (2010): 61.
5. Antoine Isaac, Robina Clayphan, and Bernhard Haslhofer, "Europeana: Moving to Linked Data," *Information Standards Quarterly* 24, no. 213 (2012): 35.
6. Digital Public Library of America, http://dp.la.
7. "Apps Library," Digital Public Library of America, http://dp.la/apps.
8. "SNAC: Social Networks and Archival Context," http://socialarchive.iath.virginia.edu.
9. Daniel V. Pitti, "Social Networks and Archival Context Project: Archival Authority Control," Social Networks and Archival Context Project, http://ica2012.ica.org/files/ pdf/Full%20papers_%20upload/ica12Fina100310.pdf.
10. Ray R. Larson and Krishna Janakiraman, "Connecting Archival Collections: The Social Networks and Archival Context Project," *Theory and Practice of Digital Libraries* 2011 (2011): 5; SNAC: Social Networks and Archival Context, http://socialarchive.iath .virginia.edu/scope.html.
11. Ibid., 6.
12. Pitti, "Social Networks and Archival Context Project," http://ica2012.ica.org/files/pdf/ Full%20papers_%20upload/ica12Fina100310.pdf.
13. "Il progetto," RELOAD, http://labs.regesta.com/progettoReload/en.
14. "L'ontologia EAC-CPF," RELOAD, http://labs.regesta.com/progettoReload/en/ lontologia-eac-cpf/; "OAD Ontology," RELOAD, http://labs.regesta.com/progettoRe load/en/oad-ontology/.

15. "Dati," Contemporary Jewish Documentation Center Foundation, http://dati.cdec.it/indiceEN.html.

16. "Shoa Vocabulary Specification Beta Version," Contemporary Jewish Documentation Center Foundation, http://dati.cdec.it/lod/shoah/reference-document.html.

17. Victor de Boer Jan Wielemaker, Judith van Gent, Marijke Oosterbroek, Michiel Hildebrand, Antoine Isaac, Jacco van Ossenbrugen, and Guus Schreiber, "Amsterdam Museum Linked Open Data," *Semantic Web* 4, no. 3 (2013): 1.

18. Ibid., 2.

19. Pedro Szekely, Craig A. Knoblock, Fengyu Yang, Xuming Zhu, Eleanor E. Fink, Rachel Allen, and Georgina Goodlander, "Connecting the Smithsonian American Art Museum to the Linked Data Cloud," *Extended Semantic Web Conference* 2013 (2013): 593.

20. Ibid., 606.

21. "Karma: A Data Integration Tool," www.isi.edu/integration/karma/.

22. "Linked Data: Smithsonian American Art Museum Announces Formation of American Art Collaborative," *Library Journal*, www.infodocket.com/2015/02/03/linked-data-smithsonian-american-art-museum-announces-formation-of-american -art-collaborative/.

23. Linked Jazz, http://linkedjazz.org.

24. "Transcript Analyzer," Linked Jazz, http://linkedjazz.org/tools/transcript-analyzer/.

25. M. Cristina Pattuelli, Matt Miller, Leanora Lange, Sean Fitzell and Carolyn Li-Madeo, "Crafting Linked Open Data for Cultural Heritage: Mapping and Curation Tools for the Linked Jazz Project," *Code4Lib Journal* no. 21, http://journal.code4lib.org/articles/8670.

26. "Ellington, Duke, 1899–1974," Library of Congress Authorities, http://authorities .loc.gov/cgi-bin/Pwebrecon.cgi?AuthRecID=2337811&v1=1&HC=9&SEQ= 20140929170541&PID=Vt5H8Yq48ZNcd22rCN_hTOC9JlZGf.

27. Seth van Hooland and Ruben Verborgh, *Linked Data for Libraries, Archives and Museums: How to Clean, Link and Publish Your Metadata* (London: Facet Publishing, 2014), 71–72.

28. "Mapping," Linked Jazz, http://linkedjazz.org/mapping/.

29. Sources of interviews include Rutgers University, Hamilton College, the Smithsonian Institution, University of Michigan, and UCLA (University of California, Los Angeles).

30. "Linked Jazz Network," Linked Jazz, http://linkedjazz.org/network/.

31. "52nd Street," Linked Jazz, http://linkedjazz.org/52ndStreet/.

32. "Relationship: A Vocabulary for Describing Relationships between People," Relationship, http://vocab.org/relationship/.html; "FOAF Vocabulary Specification 0.99," FOAF, http://xmlns.com/foaf/spec/; "MO: The Music Ontology," Music Ontology, http://musicontology.com.

33. M. C. Pattuelli, "Mapping People-Centered Properties for Linked Open Data," *Knowledge Organization* 38, no. 4 (2011): 352–59.

34. Tim Causer, Justin Tonra, and Valerie Wallace, "Transcription Maximized; Expense Minimized? Crowdsourcing and Editing *The Collected Works of Jeremy Bentham*," *Literary and Linguistic Computing* 27, no. 2 (2012): 127.

35. "https://linkedjazz.org/page/Duke_Ellington," Linked Jazz LodView, https://linkedjazz.org/page/Duke_Ellington.

36. "Linked Jazz API Documentation," Linked Jazz, http://linkedjazz.org/api/.

37. W. J. Levay, "A Semantic Makeover for CMS Data," Presentation at Code4Lib conference, February 10, 2015, Portland, Oregon, https://www.youtube.com/watch?v=gCfpQgXcpTE&feature=youtu.be&t=5m18s.

38. "Matt Miller," GitHub, https://github.com/thisismattmiller?tab=repositories.

MAKING MARC AGNOSTIC

Transforming the English Short Title Catalogue for the Linked Data Universe

Carl Stahmer

The English Short Title Catalogue (ESTC) is a union catalog and bibliography of short titles printed between 473 and 1800 in England and its former colonies or in the English language elsewhere.[1] Now more than thirty years old, the ESTC contains nearly 500,000 item records and millions of associated holding records from libraries around the world. Originally conceived and constructed as an online resource, it stands today as one of the oldest continually running digital library applications. Like most library catalogs, in its current form the ESTC is MARC-based, housed and managed in a traditional, vendor-supplied ILS. Specifically, the current ESTC runs on a technology stack consisting of an ExLibris Aleph system that provides the user interface to the catalogue, a Cuadra STAR system from the 1990s that serves as the primary records management system, and a large collection of custom-developed record manipulation scripts in a variety of programming languages. However, through the generous support of the Andrew W. Mellon Foundation, since 2011 the ESTC has been engaged in a process of reimagining itself as a "21st century research tool"—the ESTC21. (Throughout the essay, the ESTC acronym is used to refer to the ESTC as an institutional body and to the publicly available catalog. ESTC21 is used to refer to the system architecture and software that will serve as the technology stack for the new ESTC.)

PLANNING

Determining exactly what constitutes a "21st century research tool" comprised a significant portion of the project's early planning and research. Feedback on the current state of the site and on desired changes and enhancements was sought from the ESTC user base, from institutions that contribute records to the catalog, and from a range of experts in library and information sciences and the digital humanities through electronic discussion lists, an ESTC21 blog, conference presentations, and a variety of events hosted, literally, around the world. The feedback provided by users was remarkably consistent. First, it was important to most users that none of the current functionality be lost—the ESTC21 should support all of the functions of the traditional, MARC-centric OPAC. Second, when using the ESTC21, users wanted to have seamless access to information beyond, but related to, the information contained in the catalog. Third, users wanted to be able to extend the dataset represented in the catalog, capturing information about items in the catalog that lay outside the bounds of traditional bibliography, such as provenance and other forms of scholarly annotation. Additionally, whereas MARC has served the library community well since its inception in the mid-1960s, its limitations in describing non-codex historical materials such as engravings, broadsides, and postcards, to name a few, have always weighed heavily on ESTC users and catalogers. In light of this, users saw the redesign as an opportunity to move past this limitation. And finally, they universally wanted a way for end users themselves to contribute both corrections and additions to the records in the catalog.

TRIPLESTORE DATA MODEL

As an information architecture, linked data stood apart from other possible data architectures in its ability to address all of the functional requirements identified by our users. As such, the ESTC was re-architected from the ground up as a native linked data resource. Rather than crosswalk a more rigid, relational data structure into RDF as a means of exposing the catalogue as linked data, it was decided that a triplestore data model should stand at the core of the application. In this regard, the ESTC21 is designed to serve human and machine users equally. This extends to the interface level as well, as the ESTC21 provides both a web/HTML gateway for human users and an RDF gateway for machine users. Finally, the ESTC21 catalog is designed to natively expand its own offering through the ingestion of both human- (via web form submission) and machine- (via RDF linking and/or harvesting) supplied data.

The most significant advantage of a native triples data store is the ability to provide an extensible cataloging ontology. Field, relational, and XML-based data storage methodologies are gnostic in their approach to the information universe, meaning they predefine the structure of the knowledge universe as an a priori state before ingesting any data. MARC provides a strong example of this tendency, having been originally designed to stand as an electronic manifestation of the information contained on a card from a paper library catalog. Regardless of the individual variations present in any instantiation of MARC, the categories of meaning, such as author, publication data, title, and so on, constitute a predefined ontology, a formal framework, for understanding the bibliographic information universe. While this approach initially simplifies the process of associating like data with like data (e.g., an 001 field always contains a control number), it severely limits the cataloging effort when confronted with aspects of an object that do not fit appropriately into any of the defined information slots of the ontology. This limitation is familiar to all catalogers and has resulted in the increasingly verbose content of MARC 500 fields into which we have grown accustomed to throwing information on everything, including the kitchen sink. Admittedly, MARC records from institutions around the globe frequently contain information in 500 fields that could and should be more appropriately stored in other, more structured fields. However, the fact remains that with increasing frequency both catalogers and scholars are interested in capturing information for which the MARC standard simply does not account in a structured manner. This is not so much a failing of the standard as it is a reflection of the fact that good scholarship is, by definition, knowledge-producing and therefore ontologically expanding. As both librarians and scholars continue to work on the items in our catalogs, it is natural that both new information and wholly new questions (types of information) will arise; and gnostic data architectures such as MARC are inherently not flexible enough to handle this expansion.

It is worth noting here that not all linked data implementations free themselves from the ontological dilemma described above. Many RDF-based frameworks and data profiles are heavily invested in defining a particular ontological universe. This is not a bad thing. But the inherent gnosticism in frameworks such as BIBFRAME, for example, is tied to its particular RDF implementation and not to the triplestore data model itself. Rather, triplestores represent an agnostic approach to the data universe that, at least in theory, does not demand adherence to a particular ontological perspective. I do not mean to suggest that the triplestore is completely without structure, or to carry the metaphor forward, completely atheist in its orientation to the information universe. Rather, its agnostic structure is marked by the acceptance of a minimalist, general, and flexible ordering principle.

While there are, at present, many available explanations of the triplestore data model, the discussion below explicates the triplet from the particular perspective discussed above. Note that the examples provided in this explanation are made simple for expository purposes. In practice, the semantic structure of triplets can become quite complex; however, the basic tenets put forward remain true even in the face of this complexity. At the core of the triplestore is the idea that all knowledge, regardless of how abstract, compound, or complex it may be, can be represented by a series of *subject : predicate : object* statements. See figure 2.1. Thus we can, for example, say something like:

SUBJECT	PREDICATE	OBJECT
Moby Dick	Creator	Herman Melville
http://experiment.world cat.org/entity/work/ data/1930293140	http://bibframe.org/vocab/ creator	http://id.loc.gov/ authorities/names/ n79006936

Figure 2.1 | **Basic triplet structure**

This simple statement not only contains information about the relationship between the textual object titled *Moby Dick* and the person/agent named Herman Melville, but also, through its use of URI references unambiguously links both subject and object with a wider information universe. Importantly, this linking is accomplished through identification based on two distinct namespaces—the OCL works namespace (http://experiment.worldcat.org/entity/work/) and the Library of Congress name authority namespace (http://id.loc.gov/authorities/names/). A key element of linked data frameworks is that individual RDF-based ontologies and/or schemas can draw on multiple namespaces as a means of identification and disambiguation. In like fashion, individual triplet-based data stores can draw on multiple frameworks. See figure 2.2. This can be explicated by expanding our Herman Melville/*Moby Dick* statement set.

As can be seen, a wide range of information about a particular object can be captured by stringing together a series of short statements. All of this information could easily be stored in a standard MARC record. First, however, note that in the above example Herman Melville stands as both a subject and object of the triplet statement. In the triplestore universe, any subject can be an object, and any object can be a subject. This imbues data assertions with a high degree of flexibility, because a single query can return all assertions that relate to the queried entity as subject or object. Given the dataset in figure 2.2, a query on Herman Melville (http://id.loc.gov/authorities/names/n79006936) tells us both that he was the creator of *Moby Dick* (http://experiment.worldcat .org/entity/work/data/1930293140) and that his birthday was August 1, 1819. And because we have used a proper URI identifier for Herman Melville, it also links to all of the information published in the linked data universe about him.

But what happens to this linking in cases where multiple authorities exist for describing the same object or agent? For example, in addition to the Library of Congress authority record for Herman Melville (http://id.loc.gov/

SUBJECT	PREDICATE	OBJECT
Moby Dick	Creator	Herman Melville
http://experiment.world cat.org/entity/work/ data/1930293140	http://bibframe.org/vocab/ creator	http://id.loc.gov/ authorities/names/ n79006936
Herman Melvyn	Birthday	August 1, 1819
http://id.loc.gov/ authorities/names/ n79006936	http://xmlns.com/foaf/ spec/20140114.html#term _birthday	-4746816000 (Epoch Timestamp)
Moby Dick	Subject	Ship captains—Fiction
http://experiment. worldcat.org/entity/work/ data/1930293140	http://bibframe.org/vocab/ subject	http://id.loc.gov/ authorities/subjects/ sh2008111148
Moby Dick	Subject	Whaling ships—Fiction
http://experiment. worldcat.org/entity/work/ data/1930293140	http://bibframe.org/vocab/ subject	http://id.loc.gov/ authorities/subjects/ sh2008113462

Figure 2.2 | **Multiple namespaces in common data store**

authorities/names/n79006936), the Getty Research Institute also includes an entry for the same Herman Melville as part of their widely used Unified List of Artist Names (http://vocab.getty.edu/ulan/500236778). From a computing perspective, these two entities are completely distinct and unrelated. As such, a record that used the Library of Congress designator would not link to one that used the Unified List of Artist Names designator even though they in fact refer to the same individual. Organizations such as the Virtual International Authority File (VIAF) have attempted to solve this problem by providing a container URI that collects various related entities under a single URI. This is a viable solution for newly encoded resources, which can use the existing VIAF elements for their encoding. However, inserting VIAF entities into existing records is not a trivial task. Additionally, not all encoding frameworks allow VIAF references.

The triplestore data model supports an elegant solution to the above problem—the equivalency statement. An equivalency statement is a statement that creates equivalency links between instances of the same item as it is designated in multiple namespaces, thereby aligning otherwise distinct and unrelated ontologies. Consider additions to the dataset about Melville and *Moby Dick* in figure 2.3.

In relational and field-based data systems the equivalency problem involves either (1) going back through all previously cataloged data and normalizing it to an agreed-upon standard; or (2) creating and managing a complex set of linking tables and associated code. Both solutions are time- and labor-intensive and usually involve the effort of a data or software engineer. But in a triplestore universe, all that is required to solve this problem is the insertion of a single "sameAs" equivalency statement. This works because, unlike relational and field-based data models that predefine their ontologies, triplestore ontologies are defined within the data store itself. As such, they are infinitely more flexible than other data storage systems. As noted by van Hooland and Verborgh, "By adopting an extremely simple data model consisting of triples, data represented in resource description framework (RDF) becomes schema-neutral."[2] This is because the schema itself is defined as part of the triplestore. The agnostic nature of the triplestore data model thus allows us easily and without the aid of a software developer to add, modify, and/or link multiple schemas as a means of presenting and describing our data. It thus becomes possible, as shown in figure 2.3, with no programming overhead, to represent the same object in Dublin Core, BIBFRAME, EAD, Schema.org, and any other desired ontology or framework because the namespaces employed by each of these

SUBJECT	PREDICATE	OBJECT
Moby Dick	Creator	Herman Melville
http://experiment.world cat.org/entity/work/ data/1930293140	http://bibframe.org/vocab/ creator	http://id.loc.gov/ authorities/names/ n79006936
Herman Melvyn	Birthday	August 1, 1819
http://id.loc.gov/ authorities/names/ n79006936	http://xmlns.com/foaf/ spec/20140114.html#term _birthday	-4746816000 (Epoch Timestamp)
Moby Dick	Subject	Ship captains—Fiction
http://experiment.world cat.org/entity/work/ data/1930293140	http://bibframe.org/vocab/ subject	http://id.loc.gov/ authorities/subjects/ sh2008111148
Moby Dick	Subject	Whaling ships—Fiction
http://experiment.world cat.org/entity/work/ data/1930293140	http://bibframe.org/vocab/ subject	http://id.loc.gov/ authorities/subjects/ sh2008113462
Herman Melville	Is the Same as	Herman Melville
http://id.loc.gov/ authorities/names/ n79006936	http://w3.org/2002/07/ owl#sameAs	http://vocab.getty.edu/ ulan/500236778
BIBFRAME Creator	Is the Same as	Dublin Core Creator
http://bibframe.org/vocab/ creator	http://w3.org/2002/07/ owl#sameAs	http://purl.org/dc/ elements/1.1/creator

Figure 2.3 | **"Same as" ontology alignment**

frameworks can be easily aligned (through equivalency) with the namespaces already used in the data store.

Triplestore equivalence statements can be enacted at the subject or predicate level, meaning that they can apply to a single entity such as Herman Melville (<http://id.loc.gov/authorities/names/n79006936><http://w3.org/2002/07/ owl#sameAs>< http://vocab.getty.edu/ulan/500236778>), or to a predicate such as a Creator designation (<http://bibframe.org/vocab/creator><http:// w3.org/2002/07/owl#sameAs><http://purl.org/dc/elements/1.1/creator>). In cases where the equivalence relates to a subject (or a subject as the object of a predicate) the equivalence can be programmatically made to persist to all occurrences of the subject in the triplestore. The same is also true for predicate equivalence. This means that an equivalence stated one time in the triplestore will automatically take effect for all occurrences of the subject and object of the equivalence statement anywhere that they appear in the data. Thus, for example, every occurrence of http://bibframe.org/vocab/creator becomes automatically associated with http://purl.org/dc/elements/1.1/creator and vice versa.

In practice, many equivalence statements will be entered into the triple-store by a trained librarian, and as libraries move into the linked data world, one can imagine this type of work augmenting, if not ultimately replacing, the authority work currently performed by librarians. But because equivalences are themselves stated as linked data triplets, it is also likely that more Viaf-like libraries of equivalence will evolve so that individual institutions can mutually benefit from each other's equivalence efforts. The process of automated equivalence matching has also recently emerged as a potentially successful means of unearthing and instantiating triplestore equivalence. In "Aligning Ontologies with Subsumption and Equivalence Relations in Linked Data," Zong et al. outline the various opportunities presented by both human- and machine-created equivalence alignment. According to Zong et al., "Linked Data has a natural advantage for instance-based alignment," because large datasets allow for the successful application of "heuristic rules to generate subsumption and equivalence relationships based on a probability model."[3] Stated in laymen's terms, when presented with a heterogeneous dataset of the type made possible by linked data, a computer can track the various occurrences of namespace URIs in relation to each other and, from the graph of these relationships, probabilistically determine item equivalence with a degree of accuracy that falls within the error rate found in human-created data. Again, according to Zong et al., "Instance-based schema alignment methods compute the similarity between two classes by the statistic information of common instances shared by the classes, which provides a solution for the classes that are ambiguously named without globally standardized naming schemata."[4] Because the evolution of globally standardized and adopted naming schema is highly unlikely (and not truly desirable as different collections have different descriptive requirements), ontology mapping through equivalence alignment, whether performed by humans or machines, must stand at the core of any successful linked data implementation.

In light of the above, and the internal depth and richness of library catalogs, while individual triples are, by nature, simple statements, aggregated triplestores can and will quickly evolve into complex, interlinked webs, with nodes connecting both inwardly and outwardly. While the data will remain always simple at the structural level, the aggregated data store will grow quite complex. Processing such complexity at scale would have been unimaginable even a decade ago, because a significant amount of computer processing power must be directed to the task. The wide availability of such processing capacity is a relatively new phenomenon. This explains why, although visions of the semantic web have been in the community consciousness for some time, it is only now that we are beginning to see the widespread implementation of native triplet data stores.

The flexibility inherent in the triplestore data model speaks directly both to the rapidly evolving landscape of the linked data information universe and the specific desire of ESTC end users to be able to extend types of information associated with items in the ESTC catalog. As anyone who has followed the evolution of linked data since Berners-Lee and his colleagues first introduced the idea of the Semantic Web in 2001 can attest, the linked data ecosystem is a rapidly evolving one.[5] Linked data schemas change frequently by necessity as we learn more by working our way through this nascent stage of the new network infrastructure. Given this rapid state of change, any data store that is ontologically based at the structural level is doomed to a limited shelf life. The data store and all interfaces that rely on it will have to be updated every time the ontology is updated. The flexibility of an agnostic triplestore frees us from this burden, or, at a minimum, dramatically reduces the overhead involved in keeping up with this necessary and ongoing evolution.

The triplestore's flexibility also allows us to address one of the primary features requested by the ESTC user base: the ability to extend the dataset represented in the catalog, capturing information about items in the catalog that are outside the scope of traditional bibliography. Increasingly, bibliography is becoming the domain of both library professionals and subject area scholars. The mass digitization of historical documents has led to a new wave of scholarly interest in bibliographic work in a range of departments. It is now commonplace for communities of scholars to engage in debate over the production history and provenance of items in the library catalog. And catalog end users at all levels are increasingly demanding that this scholarship be available as part of the catalog. Returning to the triplets example, then, a scholar wishing to add information about source material on which Melville relied when writing *Moby Dick* might find data in figure 2.4.

In the above example, the addition of a statement about source material for *Moby Dick* immediately propagates as a result of the linked data triplestore data model to all items associated with both *Moby Dick* and the *Narrative of the Most Extraordinary and Distressing Shipwreck*. This provides invaluable data

SUBJECT	PREDICATE	OBJECT
Moby Dick http://experiment.world cat.org/entity/work/ data/1930293140	Creator http://bibframe.org/vocab/ creator	Herman Melville http://id.loc.gov/ authorities/names/ n79006936
Herman Melvyn http://id.loc.gov/ authorities/names/ n79006936	Birthday http://xmlns.com/foaf/ spec/20140114.html#term _birthday	August 1, 1819 -4746816000 (Epoch Timestamp)
Moby Dick http://experiment.world cat.org/entity/work/ data/1930293140	Subject http://bibframe.org/vocab/ subject	Ship captains—Fiction http://id.loc.gov/ authorities/subjects/ sh2008111148
Moby Dick http://experiment.world cat.org/entity/work/ data/1930293140	Subject http://bibframe.org/vocab/ subject	Whaling ships—Fiction http://id.loc.gov/ authorities/subjects/ sh2008113462
Herman Melville http://id.loc.gov/ authorities/names/ n79006936	Is the Same as http://w3.org/2002/07/ owl#sameAs	Herman Melville http://vocab.getty.edu/ ulan/500236778
BIBFRAME Creator http://bibframe.org/vocab/ creator	Is the Same as http://w3.org/2002/07/ owl#sameAs	Dublin Core Creator http://purl.org/dc/ elements/1.1/creator
Moby Dick http://experiment.world cat.org/entity/work/ data/1930293140	Is Related to http://bibframe.org/vocab/ relatedTo	*Narrative of the Most Extraordinary and Distressing Shipwreck…* http://www.worldcat.org/ oclc/795892495

Figure 2.4 | **User-enhanced triplestore**

for scholars with an interest in either text, or in any of the subject headings associated with either text.

Because of the flexibility of the triplestore data model, platform developers did not need to have a preconceived notion of the need for an "http:// bibframe.org/vocab/relatedTo" statement when the database was constructed in order for users to be able to add it to the system. The triplestore catalog can grow organically according to the needs of its user base. While it is sometimes difficult for librarians to admit, the fact is that in many cases extra-library scholars working in a particular collection are frequently more qualified than are librarians to make determinations about both what belongs in a record and record accuracy because they are able to devote more time to the in-depth study of a particularly narrow knowledge domain (in some cases as narrow as a single text). As such, collection description can be significantly improved (both in depth and accuracy) by providing the means for scholars to contribute to the bibliographic process at the record level.

TAGGING AND CONTROLLED VOCABULARIES

In the bibliographic ecosystem described above, the librarian's role again shifts from that of doing the actual describing to that of ensuring that made statements are regularized and well-formed. Inviting scholars into the catalog does not, however, come without risk. Resource scholars tend to care more about the quality of the information they are producing than they do about the quality of its presentation as a usable dataset. This is because the scholarly paper and not the record has historically been the presentation on which they are professionally judged. As a result, there is little history in academic departments of thinking about the descriptive problem itself and the need for good, regularized data. In the Semantic Web ecosystem, the tension between scholarly description and library-based bibliographic description has been both visibly and functionally born out in the space between controlled vocabularies and taxonomies. One of the first practical manifestations of the Semantic Web was the "tag cloud." As most users know, "tagging" is a system whereby users can associate any word of their choosing with a content item, and the results of this tagging are then displayed to all users as a weighted visualization of words. First implemented on a high-traffic website by the photo-sharing site Flickr in 2004, tagging and tag clouds quickly worked their way into the functional center of both traditional digital library products such as DSpace and Fedora Commons as well as less-traditional scholarly catalogs such as the Andrew W. Mellon Foundation–funded NINES initiative.[6] The arrival of folksonomic tagging was heralded as a breakthrough in description, search, and retrieval, as scholars would no longer be bound by the limited, controlled vocabularies of traditional cataloging systems. This revelatory moment was, however, short-lived, as scholars also quickly learned that things not described the same do not act the same.

The evolution from the early Semantic Web to linked data is largely marked by a return to controlled vocabularies as a means of remedying the inherent verbosity of the folksonomy. Early proponents of the Semantic Web imagined a world in which machines, with access to the vast quantities of data made available by the network, would be capable of using this context to disambiguate information and create automated links between resources with different tags and/or descriptions.[7] Experience has shown that such disambiguation is a significantly more difficult problem than was first imagined. As such, to date, completely automated efforts to link unstructured data from multiple sources have met with only limited success. Again, as noted by van Hooland and Verborgh, "The search for the Holy Grail of data integration can turn into a nightmare, in a world where anyone can state anything about anything."[8] Linking, as it turns out, is most effective when enacted on consistently normalized data. The utilization of consistent vocabularies (with persistent, reliable URIs) has, as a result, become a staple of current linked data efforts. This may seem at odds with early discussion about equivalence and ontology alignment, but the process of determining equivalence between random buckets of words and alternate, well-formed ontologies, each with its own properly defined structure, is both functionally and mathematically significant. Whereas to generate equivalence in a tag cloud environment it is necessary to calculate the relationship between every tag with every other tag, when comparing one controlled vocabulary with another, it is only necessary to consider the relationship of each item in the first vocabulary with each item in the second. This results in a significantly simplified and, hence, computational and representationally manageable comparison dataset.

SOCIAL CATALOGING

Wood, Zaidman, Ruth, and Hausenblas succinctly identify the tag cloud problem when they pose the following question, "How can anyone reuse linked data if it contains terms you've never seen before?" Indeed, the linking in linked data can only happen when data nodes can be mapped across datasets. But we need to beware of the impulse to throw out the baby with the bathwater and completely disregard folksonomic scholarly input from our users. Wood et al. answer their own question about the impossibility of linking unlike items with the astute observation that "there are two ways to make this problem tractable, one technical and the other social."[9] The technical solution to which they refer is continued effort toward automated, semantic matching. The social is the development of communities that agree to follow certain standards, schemas, and/or vocabularies in their descriptive efforts. In common parlance, we have come to refer to these social contracts as "profiles."

The development of profiles is an important practice in the establishment of common descriptive standards that function to make data functional in a linked data ecosystem. But managing the social aspect of profile development is not an easy task. It is typically accomplished through the establishment of working groups of one form or another, groups that may or may not ultimately represent the community of scholars they represent, and through various means of communication and coordination such as electronic discussion lists, blogs, meetings, and the like. Significantly, these efforts almost always take place outside of the descriptive practice itself, even when the individuals doing the descriptive work are involved in the act of profile development. The result is a necessary remove from the ground truth of the descriptive effort.

A primary goal of the ESTC21 is to resolve the separation between profile development efforts and cataloging efforts by creating a new type of catalog—one that functions simultaneously as a search and retrieval interface and as a social network that allows end users to contribute their own bibliographic work through a process of librarian-directed, social, peer review. In such a system, profile development would evolve organically as a result of the descriptive process.

Figure 2.5 presents a system diagram of the basic functionality provided by the planned ESTC21 interface.[10]

As depicted in the image, the system supports a variety of users, each with a different set of permissions. All users can search, browse, analyze, and annotate records. In this context, annotation means any type of addition of information to a record. This includes matching to an authority file through a linked data exchange with Library of Congress or VIAF, matching a holding record to an ESTC record, correcting a publication date, adding provenance information, and so on. In all cases, annotations are stored as triples in the database alongside all other data for a record. But submitted annotations do not have the status of actual record data until they pass through a system of peer and staff review. Once a user submits an annotation, it becomes available for viewing by other users who can accept or reject the correction or added information. Once an annotation receives a requisite number of yes votes, it is added to a review queue for ESTC staff librarians. When reviewing a record, ESTC staff can approve as is, approve with modification (such as, for example changing the entry to align with existing authorities, etc.), or deny

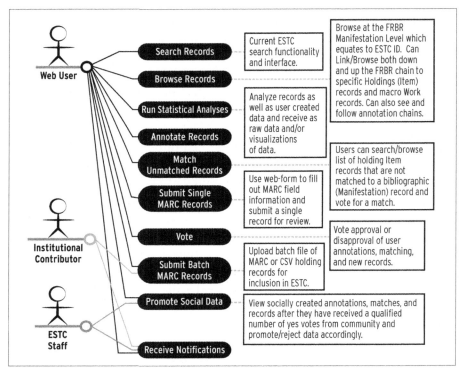

Figure 2.5 | **ESTC21 website system diagram**

with explanation. Figure 2.6 provides a state diagram showing the life cycle of a user annotation pertaining to the matching of a library holding record with an ESTC item record.

As can be seen, the entire process involves machine filtering and matching, social tagging and voting, and ESTC staff oversight as described above. This same "voting" process is applied to all end-user annotations.

A computer-assisted social cataloging practice such as the one described above offers several advantages over traditional, nonsocial methods. First, the computer can utilize the wider linked data universe to help steer user annotation as it is happening. If a user is identifying a person or place name, the system will suggest matches based on traversal of linked data authority files. For example, if a user were tagging an item as having been printed by the sixteenth-century printer John Fowler, when typing Fowler's name in the appropriate form field the system will use the VIAF API to provide auto-fill suggestions for the entry, thereby revealing the entry "John Fowler, 1537–1579." (Users can see this functionality in action directly at the viaf.org website by selecting the "Personal

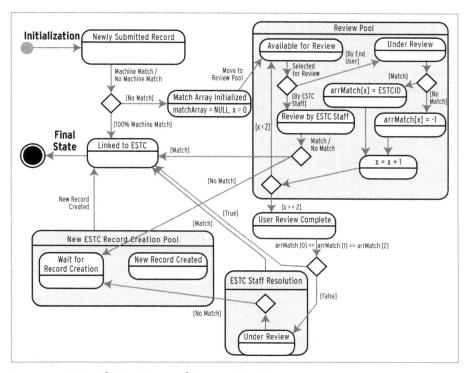

Figure 2.6 | **Social Curation and Annotation Process**

Name" option in the "Select Field" drop-down list.) Importantly, when performing this action, the user will see the name "John Fowler, 1537–1597," but what is captured by the system is the VIAF URI for this entry. This indelibly links the user's annotation to a disambiguated instance of John Fowler that will function appropriately both within the ESTC catalogue and in the wider linked data universe. This same methodology will be followed when a user is tagging a subject or identifying a holding location, in which case API calls to the appropriate Library of Congress authority files will be used to provide auto-fill information. In this way the system will exploit the wider linked data universe (as well as its own data store) to help guide end users into making the best possible, normalized decisions.

The above process works effectively when the name, subject, and so on that a user wants to identify in an annotation appear in a controlled vocabulary. But a common problem faced by catalogers when dealing with controlled vocabularies is that an item they wish to reference has no entry in the controlled vocabulary. This is particularly true for the ESTC, which catalogs a large number of nontraditional artifacts. In these cases, the creators of the annotation can suggest their own, nonassociated entry. The built-in peer review system then manages a social solution to this problem by enforcing peer agreement around the new terminology. Reviewing peers can not only approve or disapprove an annotation, they can suggest an alteration along with supporting evidence for the suggestion. This suggestion could come in the form of the identification of a controlled vocabulary link that was missed by the annotation's creator, or by the approval or suggested modification of the new entry.

Once an annotation has successfully completed its peer review process, ESTC librarians will then manage a final process of disambiguation. This can involve several courses of action. The librarian may accept one of linkages to an appropriate controlled vocabulary as suggested by peer reviewers. Similarly, the librarian may identify and implement an appropriate linkage that was missed by both the annotator and reviewers. Finally, the librarian may accept that the entry is, in fact, completely new. In such cases, the librarian will add the new entry to a local table and assign a temporary URI to the entry. This will allow the entry to function appropriately in the user interface. The librarian will submit the entry for addition to the appropriate controlled vocabulary using established procedures. When the addition life cycle is completed and a persistent URI has been assigned by the appropriate institution or agency, the temporary URI in the local system is then replaced by the permanent URI and the temporary entry removed from the local database. This entire process will be managed through the system's editorial interface, which will provide a work queue for librarians that will allow them to both track and perform the necessary steps involved in this process.

Regardless of the process by which new annotations are mapped to existing authorities or schemas, once they have passed the review of an ESTC librarian, the annotations then become part of the publicly available RDF data store, thereby providing an ever-expanding web of both internal and external linkages to both bibliographic content and the actual items being described. The machine-readable RDF face of the ESTC closes the linked data circle by exposing this web such that the scholarly work being performed within the ESTC21 interface can percolate back through the wider network of linked data. This situates the catalog as a nexus of bibliographic work in a share and share alike ecosystem in which multiple resources developed by multiple communities and individuals, each with their own particular areas of interest, are knit together at both the development and production levels through a web of relevant linkages—the value-added promise of linked data.

Notes

1. English Short Title Catalogue, estc.bl.uk.

2. Seth van Hooland and Ruben Verborgh, *Linked Data for Libraries, Archives and Museums: How to Clean, Link and Publish Your Metadata* (Chicago: Neal-Schuman, 2014), 44.

3. Nansu Zong, Sejin Nam, Jae-Hong Eom, Jinhyun Ahn, Hyunwhan Joe, and Hong-Gee Kim, "Aligning Ontologies with Subsumption and Equivalence Relations in Linked Data," *Knowledge-Based Systems* 76 (2015): 32.

4. Ibid., 41.

5. Tim Berners-Lee, James Hendler, and Ora Lassila, "The Semantic Web," *Scientific American* 284, no. 5 (May 17, 2001): 34–43.

6. "Tag Cloud," Wikipedia, October 16, 2014, http://en.wikipedia.org/wiki/Tag_cloud; see also www.dspace.org; www.fedora-commons.org; www.nines.org.

7. Berners-Lee, Hendler, and Lassila, "The Semantic Web," www.scientificamerican.com/article/the-semantic-web.

8. Van Hooland and Verborgh, *Linked Data for Libraries, Archives and Museums*, 1.

9. David Wood, Marsha Zaidman, Luke Ruth, and Michael Hausenblas, *Linked Data: Structured Data on the Web* (Shelter Island, NY: Manning Publications, 2014) 38.

10. Note that the current diagram is very MARC-centric. That is because MARC is the current format of exchange between the ESTC and its contributors. The triples data store of the ESTC21 will, however, simplify the transition to accepting records in a variety of linked data schemas.

AUTHORITY CONTROL FOR THE WEB

Integrating Library Practice with Linked Data

Allison Jai O'Dell

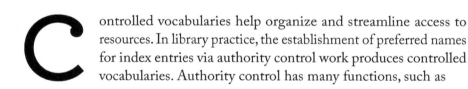

ontrolled vocabularies help organize and streamline access to resources. In library practice, the establishment of preferred names for index entries via authority control work produces controlled vocabularies. Authority control has many functions, such as

- enabling direct access to descriptive resources via index entries that correspond to search queries;
- understanding descriptive resources by clearly defining terminology, disambiguating homographs, and stating the relationships between concepts;
- enabling collocation of related resources via their shared index entries, through alphabetical filing (card catalog) or look-up links (online catalog);
- enabling data maintenance, through tracing (card catalog) or relationships (online catalog).

Linked data uses controlled vocabularies in the same ways. The call for uniform resource identifiers (URIs) in the Linked Data Principles is essentially authority control for the Web.[1] URIs, as preferred names for things, enable information access, understanding, collocation, and data maintenance. URIs also enable impromptu data merger and inferences to generate new information. The analogy of authority control—and its function in a library catalog—is an excellent way to understand linked data and the benefits it offers over other data models. Moreover, this parallel provides a framework for integrating library practice with linked data models.

In this chapter, we will review and reimagine library thesauri, metadata schemas, and information discovery, looking at how controlled vocabularies integrate library practice with linked data. We will explore existing practices that are amenable to linked data, as well as areas for expansion of best practices in a linked data environment. We begin with a discussion of value vocabularies and metadata element sets in library and linked data contexts. This is followed by a discussion of retrieval methods and discovery scenarios—built on library paradigms, and broadened to take advantage of linked data's potential. We discover that controlled vocabularies provide means for repurposing library data and library practice in linked data contexts.

VALUE VOCABULARIES

Controlled vocabularies can be used for indexing (as values) and for metadata element sets (as classes and properties). In each case, controlled vocabulary use gives meaning to data, because the data is clearly defined. In this section, we will focus on value vocabularies; in the next, we will discuss element sets.

Value vocabularies have several purposes. Notably, they serve as taxonomies, and as material for building indexes. In libraries, hierarchical thesauri define concepts and state the relationships between them. These thesauri are used to select index entries for library catalogs, enabling access to, and understanding of, library resources. Existing library thesauri, when published as linked data, bring taxonomic information to the Semantic Web, thereby enabling access to, and understanding of, web resources.

Value vocabularies are also a collocating device. When the same concept appears in two descriptions, a relationship between the descriptions can be created, with the concept as a link.[2] In library catalogs, such relationships are expressed between library holdings. On the Semantic Web, such relationships are expressed on a global scale, between anything. With the Web itself as platform, collocation occurs across domains, across platforms, and across purposes. As another benefit, linked data ontologies let us map between value vocabularies to show relationships that were previously obscured by domain-specific taxonomies.[3] Using linked data ontologies, we can be explicit that ABC in this vocabulary is the same as XYZ in that vocabulary and collocate dissimilar labels representing common things.

In a web-based, linked data environment, one further purpose for value vocabularies emerges that has hitherto been underutilized by libraries: context. Authority records in library catalogs contain a wealth of contextual information about the person, place, thing, or concept whose name is being controlled. New, descriptive elements for name authority resources under Resource Description and Access (RDA) guidelines encourage libraries to provide even more contextual information.[4] Yet, the average online library catalog does not make the content of authority records available to users.[5] The linked data principles recommend use of URLs so that these descriptive resources can be accessed and read on the Web.[6] Shifting to URLs for authority resources will make the contextualizing, biographical, and historical information captured for vocabulary control accessible to (machine and human) web users.[7] This information can be used as knowledge on those persons, topics, and so on to enhance discovery and research.

Many linked open data initiatives in libraries have begun by publishing the value vocabularies that libraries traditionally control—particularly for names, subjects, and places. Some of these are borrowed directly from existing library metadata, such as the Library of Congress Linked Data Service and OCLC's Virtual International Authority File (VIAF). Others feature a reinvigoration of authority control efforts, such as the Linked Jazz project and the Linking Lives project, which expose the social networks of persons represented in library and archives collections.[8] For another example, Bidney and Clair show that using linked data vocabularies for place names allows libraries to collocate resources by locality, connect with extended geographic information, and build cartographic representations of data.[9]

Publishing library thesauri as linked open data, and linking to other resources, adds to the growing Semantic Web. These activities provide further nodes for building a global graph of information. In particular, controlled vocabularies designed to index special collections and archives materials are likely to make the strongest contributions.[10] Because special collections and archives contain rare and unique materials, their associated controlled vocabularies are peculiar, and will augment existing linked data vocabularies with additional defined things. Analysis of existing vocabularies, and/or a demonstrated need for controlled or consistent data, can inform our efforts to publish linked data vocabularies.[11]

BEST PRACTICES

Best practices for creating library thesauri are generally transferable to linked data models, though some legacies will be reconsidered or expanded in a web environment. We will now look specifically at the library principles of uniform heading, specific entry, currency of terminology, and cross-references.[12]

The principle of a *uniform heading* declares that one point of access will bring together all representations of a single thing. For example, an author goes by various names—Al, Ally, Allison, A. J.—but these labels all represent a single person. Using a uniform heading for the variant names, or collecting them under a single URI, or else mapping the variants together in an ontology, facilitates direct access to information about that one person and all of her relationships to other things. The alternative would be several siloed graphs regarding this one person, incommunicable with each other. A difference arises here between library practice and web practice. Library data represents a closed system, and libraries have the luxury of choosing a preferred label for terminology specific to their community. By contrast, the Web assumes multiple and diverse content creators and an ever-expanding array of new information and new organizational structures.[13] Ontology design for the Semantic Web must allow for nonunique naming and duplication, but still find ways to collocate these variants. This is achieved by using URIs and equivalency references, rather than text strings. Different URI aliases for the same thing are designated as equivalent to provide uniformity for identity purposes.[14] See the discussion of cross-references below, and of ontology mapping in the following section.

The principle of a *specific entry* requires that a thing's place in a taxonomic hierarchy match the scope of the thing itself. For example, if the scope of the thing represented by "Snickerdoodle" is a cookie rolled in cinnamon, then this entry should appear in a taxonomy as narrower than "cookies." This principle remains relevant in linked data contexts and ontologies. However, in a linked data environment, we will see a change to accommodate the potential of graph modeling for data. For narrowing and collocation, library thesauri rely on tree structures, and library catalogs rely on alphabetization. The Web lets us abandon tree structures and alphabetization as retrieval mechanisms. The Web lets us, instead, build multiple, overlapping relationships between entries, which can be represented as a graph. We need no longer build increasingly narrow taxonomies—with linked data on the Web, we can explore lateral organization and relationships.[15] When publishing legacy vocabularies as linked data, it is therefore beneficial to reconsider and update relationships for a web environment. We should ask: how are these concepts represented as a network or graph?

The principle of *currency of terminology* ensures that the diction of metadata follows users' own language to bolster understanding and search recall. For example, American usage now prefers the term *cooking* over the older *cookery* (still current in British usage). Currency is often established by literary warrant—by looking at the diction of a community as expressed in its own literature. Literary warrant is based on the premise that library metadata has to do with library resources—that library data reflects the content of library resources, not the world in which they exist. When library metadata is repurposed on the Semantic Web, in contexts apart from library resources, we may need to tweak the principle of currency of terminology by reconsidering warrant. Expanding warrant to include social discourse and folksonomies will allow library vocabularies to reflect not just resources, but resource *use*.[16] Collaboration with users in thesaurus development can help libraries represent the wider social and scholarly contexts of library resources.[17]

Finally, the provision of *cross-references* between vocabulary terms is essential to building the global graph of information that linked data projects. Library thesauri include *Use/See* and *Used For (UF)* to identify preferred and alternate labels, *Broader Term (BT)* and *Narrower Term (NT)* to identify hierarchical relationships, and *Related Term (RT)/See Also* to identify other (non-hierarchical) relationships. As mentioned above, these techniques have been designed in the library community for a closed system, where taxonomies can be domain-specific, and one preferred label is chosen for each thing. On the Web, ontologies often need to reflect multiple domains and their individual semantics. Thus, Semantic Web languages extend cross-references with equivalency relationships to accommodate multiple, coexisting systems and domains. Equivalency relationships identify points of commonality between vocabularies and link vocabularies together into a graph. The translation of cross-references to a linked data environment will be discussed further in the next section on metadata element sets. Again, we will see the transition from an internal system to a global graph of information: cross-references in a linked data environment are made not just within a vocabulary, but to other vocabularies as well.

METADATA ELEMENT SETS

Librarians typically discuss controlled vocabularies as value vocabularies—that is, vocabularies to populate the content of catalog records. But controlled vocabularies are also used as metadata element sets and metadata schemas. Schemas are essentially (1) a controlled vocabulary for data elements, and (2) the ordering of these elements to lend structure to a record or triple.[18] By using a controlled vocabulary for metadata elements, machines can parse data, and understand information as humans do, within its contextual implications.

Numerous linked data element sets are available for use with library data. For example, the Bib Extend project for Schema.org, the RDA Vocabularies, FRBR Core, BIBFRAME, and the Bibliographic Ontology are specifically designed for bibliographic metadata. SKOS is ideal for subject authority data, and FOAF and BIO provide vocabularies for describing persons. The World Wide Web Consortium (W3C) offers a list of vocabularies and ontologies in common use.[19] Coyle provides an extended discussion of element sets applicable in library contexts.[20] A mix-and-match approach is appropriate using RDF as a meta-schema.[21] Ruddock illustrates that "in a bibliographic record . . . you might use the FOAF vocabulary to describe the people in the record; Dublin Core to describe title and publisher; and GeoNames to describe the place of publication."[22]

BEST PRACTICES

To determine best practices for metadata element set design, we can think analogously about value vocabulary design. If we translate the principles of uniform heading and specific entry, we find a mandate to ensure that the vocabulary is using discrete, well-defined elements, with strong integrity constraints. Translate the principle of currency of terminology, and we find a mandate to match the element set to use cases and user needs. Translate cross-references, and we find means to build relationships between elements, and between schemas.

An additional best practice for metadata element set design emerges in a linked data environment: to anticipate reuse and remixing of data. Allemang and Hendler discuss schema modeling for reuse, including suggestions to use insightful and well-formed names, pay attention to hierarchical groupings, and test the model in different contexts.[23] An important use case for remixable data is the ability to make inferences. Inferences generate new triple relationships based on existing data. Imagine two separate triple statements from two separate sources: one states that Mary lives in Honolulu, and the other states that Honolulu is in Hawaii. If a machine can match "Honolulu" in both statements, it can connect this data, and learn that Mary lives in Hawaii.

Just as linked data lets libraries connect their vocabularies with external taxonomies, so too does it allow library metadata schemas to interact with other element sets. The use of mapping properties, such as <owl:sameAs>, <owl:equivalentClass>, and <owl:equivalentProperty>, free us from domain-specific silos.[24] Such ontology mapping lets us maintain the nuance of and differences between element sets, while also expressing sameness and points of commonality. Whereas some advice encourages us to prefer element sets with widespread adoption to increase interoperability, Dunsire et al. find a growing consensus that the granularity of domain-specific element sets are important for use cases.[25] We may use the graph model of linked data to express overlap between element sets while retaining local semantic.[26]

With the graph model approach, we achieve interoperability *and* granularity.

DATA RETRIEVAL AND INFORMATION DISCOVERY

Controlled vocabularies, enhanced as linked data, facilitate expansion of old discovery scenarios and newly fashioned retrieval methods. Traditionally, libraries have enabled discovery of their metadata (and by extension, their resources) through two broad mechanisms: searching and browsing. The dual searching and browsing discovery model remains optimal in a linked data environment.[27] Meanwhile, the possible manifestations of searching and browsing platforms are vastly expanded to include intelligent searching services, dynamic display of extended content, browsing between and among domains, and creative visualizations of data elements and their relationships. In the following paragraphs, we discuss how the searching and browsing discovery model can be harnessed and expanded to create new tools with linked data technologies.

Linked data lays groundwork for cross-collection searching by relating resources in different library silos. Existing solutions for indexing data from multiple collections often compromise the richness of distinctive metadata, because they transform data from one schema to another and necessarily "dumb it down" to produce interoperability.[28] Instead, linked data ontology mapping allows us to maintain the integrity of different elements while establishing points of commonality. The result is granular, cross-collection search capability.

Linked data lets us extend search results beyond the library's resources, which can provide contextual information, ameliorate failed searches, and inspire further exploration. Library holdings cannot encompass the totality of information available, and library metadata cannot fully represent all aspects of every resource. Several projects demonstrate how linked datasets supplement library search results with additional information, for instance: to provide publication histories for serials; to expand biographical information about authors; to relate component parts to their wholes—such as articles in journals—or manual objects to digitized counterparts; to collect and share user-generated content; or to furnish access to reception histories and cultural context.[29] These supplemented search results are generated using controlled vocabularies, because (1) controlled vocabularies are the mechanism by which resources are linked together, and (2) the taxonomic information accessed at HTTP URIs confers information about people, places, topics, and so on.[30]

SPARQL—a query language for data stored in the RDF format—lets power users search library data how they choose. The online library catalog, as we know it, requires users to visit a catalog interface to access data. The catalog interface allows users to build structured queries of database content without a query language, but effectively limits the number of query options available. Instead, a SPARQL end point expands the ways that users can search and access library data. Controlled vocabularies—as both values and metadata elements—let SPARQL users know what to look for. SPARQL users may include savvy researchers, developers, and web content writers, resulting in the appearance of library data in nonlibrary resources.

Linked data paves the way for library data to appear in web search engine results. So long as library data exists as part of the deep web—the content that bots cannot crawl and index for search engines—library data remains hidden from most exploratory searches. The use of controlled vocabularies in linked data formats helps bots understand data by placing data within its semantic contexts. When bots understand data, they can successfully index it for search engines.

Furthermore, this semantic context enables semantic search. Semantic search technology relates user search queries to their probable intent, thereby offering more relevant results.[31] This technology is built on a combination of understanding what humans intend (e.g., through natural language processing and concept matching) and understanding data (e.g., through well-parsed, well-defined, controlled vocabularies). Rather than matching search query strings to data strings, semantic search technology is about machine understanding of the relationship between search queries and data. Systems that understand ontological relationships can deliver better results, make suggestions for users, and help them to improve their search strategies.[32]

Linked data provides a framework for new and exciting browsing experiences.[33] Browsing in libraries has historically been facilitated by (1) shelf browsing, offered through classification numbers, and (2) index browsing, offered through controlled vocabularies. There is a bias towards thinking of browsing as a manual activity.[34] But in a web-based environment, browsing need not be limited to classification and alphabetical indexes.[35] The Web opens up virtual browsing possibilities, such as auto-suggestions, faceted navigation tools, and data visualizations, to encourage curiosity, attract exploration of resources, and suggest pathways to learning.[36] In a linked data environment, controlled vocabularies can make index browsing a dynamic, engaging, and visual experience. Moreover, this browsing can be carried out by follow-your-nose behavior, or "surfing."[37] In follow-your-nose style browsing, users navigate laterally through the information universe by clicking links for related things.[38] Controlled vocabularies supply the nodes for identifying commonalities and building these links.[39.] It is Cutter's collocation principle, employed as an endless web of relationships, rather than a single point of commonality.[40]

BEST PRACTICES

In a linked data environment, controlled vocabularies continue to support data retrieval and information discovery. Best practices for searching and browsing platform design will remain relevant. But we will need to tweak our approaches when library resources are linked to external resources, and when library data is truly available on the Web. In a linked data environment, best practices for enabling data retrieval and discovery should anticipate the global graph of information, ensuring (1) that library data will be found outside of libraries, and (2) that library users have access to more than library data.

CONCLUSION

Because of the overlap between the library concept of authority control and the Linked Data Principles library controlled vocabularies, and associated best practices, are transferable to linked data contexts. Using library thesauri and metadata schemas in linked data formats enables information access, understanding, and collocation, as well as data maintenance, merger, and inferencing to be undertaken on the Web. The principles of uniform heading, specific entry, currency of terminology, and cross-references from library thesaurus design are applicable to linked data, if we shift our approaches and expectations to a global scale—taking advantage of web and Semantic Web technologies to build a global graph of information.

The searching and browsing model of library discovery is also transferable to linked data contexts. On the Semantic Web, controlled vocabularies can enable information use and discovery across collections, across domains, and across the globe. Possibilities include expansion of search results to include linked data sources, semantic search technology that understands users' intent, full control of search queries through SPARQL end points, browsing laterally through a networked graph of information, and browsing between datasets and domains.

This chapter has reviewed library thesauri, metadata schemas, and information discovery, looking at how controlled vocabularies integrate library practice with linked data. We have identified existing practices that are amenable to linked data, as well as areas for expansion of best practices in a linked data environment. This discussion helps us to transition library data into linked data, and begin imagining possibilities for library data modeling and discovery on the Semantic Web.

Notes

1. Tim Berners-Lee, "Linked Data: Design Issues," *W3C* (June 18, 2009), www.w3.org/DesignIssues/LinkedData.html.
2. Arlene G. Taylor, *The Organization of Information* (Santa Barbara, CA: Libraries Unlimited, 2003), 312–13.
3. Amy J. Barton et al., "A Case Study of a Semantically Enhanced Public Health Digital Collection," *Journal of Library Metadata* 13, no. 4 (2013): 367–80.
4. Stephen Davison et al., "Enhancing an OAI-PMH Service Using Linked Data: A Report from the Sheet Music Consortium," *Journal of Library Metadata* 13, nos. 2–3 (2013): 141–62.
5. Allison Jai O'Dell, "Book Artists Unbound: Providing Access to Creator Metadata with EAC-CPF," *Art Documentation* 33, no. 2 (2014): 267–78.
6. Getaneh Alemu et al., "Linked Data for Libraries: Benefits of a Conceptual Shift from Library-Specific Record Structures to RDF-Based Data Models," *New Library World* 113, nos. 11–12 (2012): 549–70.

7. Tom Heath and Christian Bizer, *Linked Data: Evolving the Web into a Global Data Space* (California: Morgan & Claypool, 2011), 2–3.

8. M. Cristina Pattuelli, "Personal Name Vocabularies as Linked Open Data: A Case Study of Jazz Artist Names," *Journal of Information Science* 38, no. 6 (2012): 558–65; Jane Stevenson, "Linking Lives: Creating an End-User Interface Using Linked Data," *Information Standards Quarterly* 24, nos. 2–3 (2012): 14–23.

9. Marcy Bidney and Kevin Clair, "Harnessing the Geospatial Semantic Web: Toward Place-Based Information Organization and Access," *Cataloging & Classification Quarterly* 52, no. 1 (2014): 69–76.

10. Barton et al., "A Case Study of a Semantically Enhanced Public Health Digital Collection," 367–80.

11. Petra Pejsova, Tereza Simandlova, and Jindrich Mynarz, "A Linked-Data Vocabulary of Grey Literature Document Types: Version 1.0," presented at the International Conference on Grey Literature (2012), http://ozk.unizd.hr/proceedings/index.php/lida/article/download/87/55.

12. Lois Mai Chan, *Cataloging and Classification: An Introduction* (Lanham, MD: Scarecrow, 2007), 198–206.

13. For discussion of the open world assumption, see Dean Allemang and Jim Hendler, *Semantic Web for the Working Ontologist: Effective Modeling in RDFS and OWL* (Amsterdam: Morgan Kaufmann, 2009).

14. Heath and Bizer, *Linked Data*, 2.2.

15. Alice Thudt, Uta Hinrichs, and Sheelagh Carpendale, "The Bohemian Bookshelf: Supporting Serendipitous Book Discoveries through Information Visualization," *CHI '12: Proceedings of the SIGCHI Conference on Human Factors in Computing Systems* (2012), 1461–70, "Design for Serendipity through Visualization."

16. Scott A. Golder and Bernardo A. Huberman, "Usage Patterns of Collaborative Tagging Systems," *Journal of Information Science* 32, no. 2 (2006): 198–208; Louise F. Spiteri, "The Use of Folksonomies in Public Library Catalogues," *Serials Librarian* 51, no. 2 (2006): 75–89.

17. Michael K. Buckland, "Obsolescence in Subject Description," *Journal of Documentation* 68, no. 2 (2012): 154–61.

18. An extended explanation of data models and schema design is Erik T. Mitchell, "Building Blocks of Linked Open Data in Libraries," in *Library Linked Data: Research and Adoption* (Chicago: Library Technology Reports, July 2013).

19. W3C, "Common Vocabularies/Ontologies/Micromodels" (2014), www.w3.org/wiki/TaskForces/CommunityProjects/LinkingOpenData/CommonVocabularies.

20. Karen Coyle, "Metadata Elements," in *Linked Data Tools: Connecting on the Web* (Chicago: Library Technology Reports, May/June 2012).

21. Mitchell, "Building Blocks of Linked Open Data in Libraries."

22. Bethan Ruddock, "Linked Data and the LOCAH Project," *Business Information Review* 28, no. 2 (June 2011): 107.

23. Allemang and Hendler, *Semantic Web for the Working Ontologist*, 271–91.

24. Ruddock, "Linked Data and the LOCAH Project," 105–11.

25. Jeff Mixter, "Using a Common Model: Mapping VRA Core 4.0 into an RDF Ontology," *Journal of Library Metadata* 41, no. 1 (2014): 1–23; Ruddock, "Linked Data and the LOCAH Project"; Gordon Dunsire et al., "Linked Data Vocabulary Management: Infrastructure Support, Data Integration, and Interoperability," *Information Standards Quarterly* 24, nos. 2–3 (2012): 4–13.

26. Dunsire et al., "Linked Data Vocabulary Management," 9.

27. Cory K. Lampert and Silvia B. Southwick, "Leading to Linking: Introducing Linked Data to Academic Library Digital Collections," *Journal of Library Metadata* 13, nos. 2–3 (2013): 230–53.

28. Thomas Johnson, "Indexing Linked Bibliographic Data with JSON-LD, BibJSON and Elasticsearch," *Code4Lib* 19 (January 15, 2013), http://journal.code41ib.org/articles/7949.

29. Marlene van Ballegooie and Juliya Borie, "From Record-Bound to Boundless: FRBR, Linked Data, and New Possibilities for Serials Cataloging," *The Serials Librarian: From the Printed Page to the Digital Age* 66, nos. 1–4 (2014): 76–87; Heather Lea Moulaison and Susan Nicole Stanley, "Beyond Failure: Potentially Mitigating Failed Author Searches in the Online Library Catalog Through the Use of Linked Data," *Journal of Web Librarianship* 7, no. 1 (2013): 37–57; Laura Krier, "Serials, FRBR, and Library Linked Data: A Way Forward," *Journal of Library Metadata* 12, no. 2–3 (2012): 177–87.

30. Ragnhild Holgerson, Michael Preminger, and David Massey, "Using Semantic Web Technologies to Collaboratively Collect and Share User-Generated Content in Order to Enrich the Presentation of Bibliographic Records: Development of a Prototype Based on RDF, D2RQ, Jena, SPARQL and WorldCat's FRBRization Web Service," *Code4Lib* 17 (June 1, 2012), http://journal.code41ib.org/articles/6695.

31. Kaisa Hypen, "Kirjasampo: Rethinking Metadata," *Cataloging & Classification Quarterly* 52, no. 2 (2014): 156–80.

32. Fiona Bradley, "Discovering Linked Data," *Library Journal* 132, no. 7 (April 15, 2009): 49.

33. Junzhong Gu, "Semantics Oriented Web Searching," *International Journal of Database Theory and Application* 6, no. 4 (2013): 15–26.

34. Thea Lindquist et al., "Using Linked Open Data to Enhance Subject Access," *Cataloging & Classification Quarterly* 51, no. 8 (2013): 913–28.

35. Toby Burrows, "A Machine for Browsing: Beyond the 'Single Search Box,'" *OCLC Systems & Services: International Digital Library Perspectives* 28, no. 1 (2012): 56–58.

36. Karen Calhoun, "Being a Librarian: Metadata and Metadata Specialists in the Twenty-first Century," *Library Hi Tech* 25, no. 2 (2007): 174–87.

37. Kate M. Joranson, Steve VanTuyl, and Nina Clements, "E-Browsing: Serendipity and Questions of Access and Discovery," *Charleston Library Conference* (Purdue University: Purdue e-Pubs, 2013).

38. Thudt, Hinrichs, and Carpendale, "The Bohemian Bookshelf: Supporting Serendipitous Book Discoveries through Information Visualization," 1461–70.

39. Ed Summers, "Following Your Nose to the Web of Data," *Inkdroid: Paper or Plastic?* (January 4, 2008), http://inkdroid.org/journal/2008/01/04/following-your-nose-to-the-web-of-data.

40. Charles Ammi Cutter, *Rules for a Dictionary Catalog*, 4th ed. (Washington, DC: Government Printing Office, 1904); Leigh Dodds and Ian Davis, "Linked Data Patterns: A Pattern Catalogue for Modelling, Publishing, and Consuming Linked Data" (2012), Chapter 6, Application Patterns, Follow Your Nose, http://patterns.dataincubator.org/book/follow-your-nose.html.

LINKED DATA IMPLICATIONS FOR AUTHORITY CONTROL AND VOCABULARIES

An STM Perspective

Iker Huerga and Michael P. Lauruhn

S cience, technical, and medical publishing (STM) and research communications are constantly evolving. At present, there are numerous constraints, pressures, and opportunities affecting stakeholders at all levels, be they publishers, researchers, librarians, or administrators. Currently, stakeholders are transitioning away from traditional roles where researchers researched and created findings, publishers published and distributed findings, and libraries made findings available to their patrons and served as archives and repositories. Instead, the emergence of key technologies and networks has created a developing ecosystem for sharing research findings that is no longer confined to the journal article model. In the emerging model, more pressure will be put on all stakeholders to become data providers and content creators. Likewise, there will be more opportunities for all stakeholders to develop applications that can consume, map, and interpret data and content and make it actionable for reuse by various audiences.

Two key components in making data and content ready to be consumed across networks and disciplines are making sure that objects and concepts are identifiable and that the metadata generated is interoperable. This is particularly important in the space of research communications for STM publishing. Significant policy changes from funders are mandating that data from publicly funded research be made open. A 2013 policy memorandum from the Obama administration requires federal agencies with large research and development budgets "to develop plans to make the published results of federally funded research freely available to the public within one year of publication and requir[e] researchers to better account for and manage the digital data resulting from federally funded scientific research."[1] Many institutes and centers within the National Institutes of Health have their own data-sharing policies.[2] In addition, some nongovernmental funders and new publishing models are also devising policies focused on making research data available.[3]

Secondly, there is a growing insistence that science reported in findings should be reproducible. This is because recent studies have shown that scientific findings that are published in journals often lack the detail and information needed to reproduce the experiments described in them. Among the most notable of those studies:

> Begley and Ellis selected 53 published articles representing landmark studies (defined as research that showed "something completely new" including new approaches to "targeting cancers or alternative clinical uses for existing therapeutics"). The findings described were able to be confirmed in only 6 of the 53 cases.[4]
>
> Prinz, Schlange, and Asadullah reviewed 47 projects related to oncology and found only about 20 to 25 percent of the projects had relevant published data that was precisely consistent with their in-house findings, and almost two-thirds had inconsistencies between published data and in-house data.[5]
>
> Vasilevsky et al. describe their attempts to precisely identify resources as they appeared in published articles. Resources are defined as the research resources needed to reproduce an experiment. These include model organisms, antibodies, knockdown reagents such as RNAi, and cell lines. In their findings, 54 percent of resources could not be uniquely identified from the publication the research was described in, "regardless of domain, journal impact factor, or reporting requirements."[6]

This setting provides a real opportunity for librarians and information administrators to develop services that can assist researchers on the front lines to be better stewards of their data. Librarians in medical and scientific organizations are uniquely positioned to help their researchers understand what vocabulary resources are available to them and the significance of using them to better annotate their data. It also provides an opportunity for linked data registries to provide access to resources that are sustainable and interoperable. While it is likely that one may never need to formally identify something as precise as antibodies and reagents, the above examples show where precise identification of objects that are published is crucial. But even if one is dealing with persons, animals, places, institutions, books, or other objects of a less scientific nature, making connections to available resources can enhance one's work and allow others to benefit from it.

Linked data offers several opportunities for content and data curators to enhance their content by allowing it to interact with external data and content in innovative and robust ways. Already, there are examples of how bibliographic metadata can be used in a linked data environment to enhance discovery services for library users, so that they can go beyond the immediate collection they are searching and find new resources from outside. Also, online publishers are taking advantage of Wikipedia and DBpedia to create linkages to key concepts in articles and provide readers with background information through definitions, data, and other supplemental resources.

It is expected that more resources will be made available as linked data in the near future. In the United States, the National Library of Medicine has a linked data Infrastructure team exploring beta releases of both Medical Subject Headings (MeSH) (http://hhs.github.io/meshrdf/) and PubChem (https://pubchem.ncbi.nlm.nih.gov/rdf/) in RDF. Likewise, organizations like Elsevier have been developing taxonomy models such as the Elsevier Merged Medical Taxonomy (EMMeT). EMMeT provides mapping of concepts from major medical taxonomies and facilitates content enrichment of content assets.[7]

But what steps must be taken to create these linkages so that they can be implemented accurately and reliably? They include a blend of traits from traditional library cataloging, knowledge about current standards in the linked data and Semantic Web environment, and the ability to understand use cases and make critical evaluations about resources that are appropriate and sustainable.

AUTHORITY CONTROL AND VOCABULARY'S ROLE IN LINKED DATA

Authority control is a classic library science discipline and organizing principle that mandates that individual concepts be given unique labels. The emphasis is on the notion that the same label is not shared by multiple concepts. Librarians use authority control in the area of descriptive cataloging and when assigning subject metadata to objects within the library collection so that they can be retrieved by systems ranging from card catalogs to online public access catalogs (OPACs) to more recent search and information retrieval systems.

In the 1960s machine-readable cataloging (MARC) was developed as a data format that would allow computers to exchange, use, and interpret bibliographic information. (www.loc.gov/marc/faq.html). The results of MARC records being disseminated is not what we would consider "interoperability" by current standards. They were used primarily to share records among libraries and library consortia in order to reduce cataloging costs and support the sharing of resources. MARC allowed for the work of individuals to be shared with thousands. It was also consistent with the library community's "long and rich history of using technology to realize economies of scale." While the MARC format was focused on catalog records and the information retrieval technology of the time, current components of the Semantic Web allow for a much more mature form of interoperability, with two significant differences: the ability to take information (data and content) and repurpose it from its original intent, and the ability to expand and map between vocabularies.

Librarians use controlled vocabularies that serve as classification schemas when assigning labels. The best-known example of a controlled vocabulary in American libraries is the Library of Congress Subject Headings (LCSH). In the case of people, places, and organizations, the Library of Congress Name Authority File (LCNAF) provides access to millions of concepts.

LCNAF requires unique labels to describe objects. Personal names are frequently in need of disambiguation, and library catalogers use authority control within LCNAF to disambiguate them. In the case of personal names, it is common to add middle names or middle initials to names, or other information such as birth and death year or an occupational term such as "Shipmaster" to render the label unique. See figure 4.1.

Places that share the same name are also distinguished from one another by adding information about which place the label—and works—that it is applied to. See figure 4.2.

6.	Smith, L. J. (Leslie John), 1881-1968	LC Name Authority File	Personal Name	no2008100100
	Smith, Leslie John, 1881-1968			
7.	Smith, J. L. (John Lewis), 1941-	LC Name Authority File	Personal Name	n80156730
	Smith, John Lewis, 1941-			
8.	Smith, John L. (John Lyman), 1828-1898	LC Name Authority File	Personal Name	nr2006017291
9.	Smith, John L. (John Lyle), 1964-	LC Name Authority File	Personal Name	n00010192
10.	Smith, John L., 1938-	LC Name Authority File	Personal Name	no2009120414
11.	Smith, John L., 1960-	LC Name Authority File	Personal Name	n95032191
12.	Smith, John L., 1920-	LC Name Authority File	Personal Name	n79138497
13.	Smith, John K. L.	LC Name Authority File	Personal Name	n2002070985
14.	Smith, John L., 1945-	LC Name Authority File	Personal Name	n99275041
15.	Smith, John L. (Shipmaster)	LC Name Authority File	Personal Name	n2003087148
16.	Smith, John L.	LC Name Authority File	Personal Name	n84159044

Figure 4.1 | **Example LCNAF results from Library of Congress names**

1.	Riverside Federation of Republican Women (Riverside, Calif.)	LC Name Authority File	Corporate Name	nr2006028846
	Riverside RWF (Riverside, Calif.) ; Riverside Republican Women's Federation (Riverside, Calif.) ; California Federation of Republican Women. Riverside Federation of Republican Women			
2.	Riverside Unified School District (Riverside County, Calif.)	LC Name Authority File	Corporate Name	n85176793
	Riverside County (Calif.). Riverside Unified School District ; Riverside Unified School District			
3.	Riverside County Administrative Office	LC Name Authority File	Corporate Name	n82206222
	Riverside County (Calif.). Administrative Office ; Riverside County (Calif.). Riverside County Administrative Office			
4.	Riverside ECHG (Organization)	LC Name Authority File	Corporate Name	nb2012018929
	Riverside Group. Riverside ECHG			
5.	City of Riverside Redevelopment Agency	LC Name Authority File	Corporate Name	n82213544
	Riverside (Calif.). Redevelopment Agency ; Riverside Redevelopment Agency			
6.	Riverside (Calif.). Office of the City Manager	LC Name Authority File	Corporate Name	no97045400
	Riverside (Calif.). City Manager, Office of the ; Riverside (Calif.). City Manager			

Figure 4.2 | **Example LCSH results from Library of Congress names**

Traditionally, most libraries have used LCSH as the core controlled vocabulary to enforce authority control in subjects. It is important to realize that much of the planning, development, and evolution of LCSH—and many other classic controlled subject vocabularies—did not occur with Internet-based technologies in mind. Most were developed to support the card catalog that was ubiquitous in libraries during most of the twentieth century, and which was eventually superseded by the MARC-based OPAC.

The problem with this traditional approach was that it did not provide a decentralized way of sharing and reusing existing vocabularies. In the event that one of the terms would need to be changed, for example, Expo 67 (Montréal, Québec) [AACR2] to Expo (International Exhibitions Bureau) (1967 : Montréal, Québec), the only way a third party could note this change would be by downloading the modified authority record and using it to update access points in their own system. This was a potentially time-consuming, manual, and error-prone approach.

For several years, people have argued that these authority records have a larger role in a web-based environment. This case can be made even stronger as Semantic Web tools become more mature and prominent in data and content transfer. As Corey Harper and Barbara Tillett observed, "Authority records, library thesauri, and library controlled vocabularies, if converted into formats that support Semantic Web technologies, have an even greater potential for revolutionizing the way users—and machines—interact with information on the Internet."[8] The following section describes how such Semantic Web technologies—and URIs in particular—solve that decentralization problem.

AUTHORITY CONTROL VOCABULARIES USING URIS

To people who are used to managing content and data in databases, descriptive labels associated with URIs often appear to be clunky and long. While this might be the case, it is important to recognize that these labels play a significant role in the evolution of unique identifiers and unique identification systems that make the Semantic Web and linked data possible. See figure 4.3 for Wikipedia URLs that represent articles on various "Riversides" and "John Smiths." These URLs are similar to the variety of LCNAF labels in figures 4.1 and 4.2.

Most people would look at the list above and agree that it is a list of uniform resource locators (URLs) used to access a web page. However, URLs are also a type of URI (uniform resource identifier), and URIs are unique in the same way that the entries and labels in traditional controlled vocabularies are unique. URIs are used to identify the names of "resources"—all of the things, concepts, and entities represented in the Semantic Web.

Many examples exist of vocabularies that were conceived and published before the advent of the World Wide Web. For example, the AGROVOC thesaurus was initially published by the Food and Agriculture Organization of the United Nations in the early 1980s. It was intended to be used as a

http://en.wikipedia.org/wiki/Riverside,_Iowa

http://en.wikipedia.org/wiki/wiki/Riverside,_Charles_County,_Maryland

http://en.wikipedia.org/wiki/wiki/Riverside,_Harford_County,_Maryland

http://en.wikipedia.org/wiki/wiki/Riverside,_Cambridge

http://en.wikipedia.org/wiki/wiki/Riverside_(Duluth)

http://en.wikipedia.org/wiki/wiki/Riverside,_Missouri

http://en.wikipedia.org/wiki/wiki/Riverside,_Nevada

http://en.wikipedia.org/wiki/wiki/Riverside,_Paterson,_New_Jersey

http://en.wikipedia.org/wiki/wiki/Riverside,_Buffalo,_New_York

http://en.wikipedia.org/wiki/wiki/Riverside,_Steuben_County,_New_York

---

http://en.wikipedia.org/wiki/John_Smith_(Canadian_poet)

http://en.wikipedia.org/wiki/John_Smith_(actor)

http://en.wikipedia.org/wiki/John_N._Smith

http://en.wikipedia.org/wiki/John_Smith_(English_filmmaker)

http://en.wikipedia.org/wiki/John_F._Smith

http://en.wikipedia.org/wiki/John_Smith_(comics)

http://en.wikipedia.org/wiki/John_Gibson_Smith

http://en.wikipedia.org/wiki/John_Smith_(musician)

http://en.wikipedia.org/wiki/John_Smith_(Conservative_politician)

http://en.wikipedia.org/wiki/John_Smith,_Baron_Kirkhill

Figure 4.3 | **Wikipedia URLs**

controlled vocabulary for indexing publications about agricultural science and technology, particularly for indexing the bibliographic records that comprise the International System for Agricultural Science and Technology database.[9] In 2000 AGROVOC abandoned paper printing and went digital, with data storage handled by a relational database. In 2004 a conversion to Web Ontology Language (OWL) was tested, and in 2009 AGROVOC was made available as linked data in RDF/SKOS-XL.[10]

URIs provide a mechanism to identify resources. A resource can be anything that has its own identity—things, human beings, cities, and so on. The Web also provides the hypertext transfer protocol (HTTP) to retrieve representations of these resources. The Web typically uses URLs to identify the network "locations" of these resources. However, URIs and URLs are not identical.

Let's illustrate the difference between URIs and URLs with one example: New York City as represented in DBpedia. DBpedia (http://dbpedia.org) extracts structured information from Wikipedia and makes it available on the Web following the Linked Data Principles as a five-star linked open data service (www.w3.org/DesignIssues/LinkedData.html).

The resource (URI) that uniquely represents New York City inside DBpedia is http://dbpedia.org/resource/New_York_City. When we try to retrieve a representation for this resource by putting this URI in a web browser, we will be redirected to its HTML representation at a slightly different URL and presented with a version intended for human rather than machine consumption, listing all the properties (e.g., population, area, form of government) and related values: http://dbpedia.org/page/New_York_City.

One of the main advantages of this approach is that this uniquely identified resource, New York City, can now be retrieved in a decentralized way by machine using web technologies. For instance, if tomorrow DBpedia decides to add information about the population distribution in New York City, a third party using DBpedia won't need to get the latest version of the data for New York City and update it into their local copy. Because one single resource (URI) for New York City exists, all the changes made to it will be automatically propagated.

Therefore, URIs are a natural fit to represent resources in authority control vocabularies, and as we have seen, big initiatives like DBpedia have already adopted them.

But how can we create URIs? Which language should we use for this? And even more important, how can we add semantic relationships between different resources? To answer all these questions, the World Wide Web Consortium (W3C) (http://w3.org) developed a standard called RDF (resource description framework).

RDF

RDF (www.w3.org/RDF) is a general-purpose language developed by W3C for representing and describing information on the Web. For the context of this chapter, this information will consist of controlled vocabularies.

The key data structures for RDF are (1) subject-predicate-object (SPO) triples and (2) graphs. An SPO triple represents a single assertion about a resource while an RDF graph comprises a set of triples.

Taking the New York City URI as an example, an RDF triple would be the one in the figure below, which can be read as, the URI http://dbpedia.org/ resource/New_York_City (subject) has a label (rdf:label, predicate), "New York City" (predicate). Furthermore, the predicate is represented in English (@en):

http://dbpedia.org/resource/New_York_City	rdfs:label	"New York City"@en

Another representation of RDF triples, using XML for serialization, is also widespread on the Web. The RDF assertion in the example above can be represented in RDF/XML presented below:

```
<rdf:RDF xmlns:rdf="http://www.w3.org/1999/02/22-rdf-syntax-ns#">
<dbpedia-owl:City rdf:about="http://dbpedia.org/resource/New_York_City"
xmlns:dbpedia-owl="http://dbpedia.org/Ontology/">
<rdfs:label xml:lang="en" xmlns:rdfs="http://www.w3.org/2000/01/rdf-schema#">
New York City
</rdfs:label>
</dbpedia-owl:City>
</rdf:RDF>
```

The content in these two figures make the same assertion about the resource (New York City) in the same manner. The only difference is that in (1) the RDF triple is serialized using the N-Triples serialization format, whereas (2) uses RDF/XML.

As we can observe, RDF/XML is much more verbose, and more space is needed to make the same assertions about a resource. The main reason that RDF/XML is widely used as a serialization is because many organizations—and publishers in particular—have developed XML-based tools over the last several years, making it is easier for them to handle RDF serialized as XML.

RDF is rapidly becoming the mainstream language for representing authority control vocabularies in a more web-friendly manner in most scenarios. But some use cases exist in which the semantics of RDF are not sufficient. For those cases, W3C developed the Web Ontology Language (OWL) that provides an extra level of expressivity for controlled vocabularies.

OWL

OWL is a set of knowledge representation languages that allow the creation of formal semantic controlled vocabularies, also called ontologies.

OWL provides mechanisms to add a set of semantic constraints and properties that would not be possible otherwise. For example, we can consider a very broad resource like human being or Person. DBpedia uses the resource http://dbpedia.org/resource/Person to represent a person on the Web. The representation of this resource covers its name, a set of notes about the resource, and so on. This information is probably enough for most use cases, but what if we want to go one step further? What if, for example, we would like to assert that every person has two and only two parents?

With RDF alone, we would not be able to add this type of semantics to our vocabulary. We would need OWL, and more specifically a set of cardinality constraints that OWL provides.

Using RDF/XML, the representation of these constraints is illustrated below:

```
<owl:Restriction>
<owl:onProperty rdf:resource="#hasParent" />
<owl:maxCardinality rdf:datatype="&xsd;nonNegativeInteger">2</owl:maxCardinality>
<owl:minCardinality rdf:datatype="&xsd;nonNegativeInteger">2</owl:minCardinality>
</owl:Restriction>
```

The XML above states the property "hasParent" has two cardinality constraints—one for a maximum and another one for a minimum number of parents: 2.

In this way OWL provides a straightforward way to add more formal semantics to those controlled vocabularies that require it. In fact, different publishers and libraries have adopted both RDF and OWL as formal languages to represent their knowledge organization schemes. But a new problem has arisen. There are cases in which organizations have different URIs to represent the same resource under their own domain. For instance, the geographical database Geonames, www.geonames.org (which also adopted RDF and OWL to represent their vocabularies on the Web), uses the URI www.geonames .org/5128581 to represent New York City, whereas DBpedia uses a different URI, http://dbpedia.org/resource/New_York_City.

This can happen with multiple vocabularies from different organizations, making the problem even bigger as more and more publishers and libraries adopt these technologies to represent their controlled vocabularies.

Fortunately, there are mechanisms that allow us to create mappings across multiple vocabularies, making assertions about two or more URIs that actually refer to the same resource. In the next section we will describe two of the most widely used methods in more depth.

MAPPING VOCABULARIES

A mapping is defined as a single relation between two concepts from two different controlled vocabularies. These relations are categorized based on their type. For instance, if we would like to assert that concept A in vocabulary A' has a similar definition to concept B in vocabulary B' but is more general in scope, we could use the relation skos:broaderMatch, and the RDF triple of this relation is found below:

B':conceptB	skos:broaderMatch	A':conceptA

In certain cases, we will need to establish a relation between two concepts from different controlled vocabularies that asserts that they are equivalent. One of the most widely used mechanisms to do so is owl:sameAs. The predicate owl:sameAs is used to assert that two individuals (instances in the context of OWL) are the same. Therefore the two URIs, each from a different controlled vocabulary, refer to the same resource.

If we would like to state that the term "New York City" from the controlled vocabulary of Geonames and the term "New York City" from DBpedia, which we presented in the previous section, actually refer to the same resource (the City of New York), we would use the RDF triple below:

http://www.geonames.org/5128581	owl:sameAs	http://dbpedia.org/resource/New _York_City

This would be serialized as RDF/XML shown below:

```
<rdf:Description rdf:about="http://www.geonames.org/5128581">
<owl:sameAs rdf:resource="http://dbpedia.org/resource/New_York_City"/>
</rdf:Description>
```

The practical implications of this statement would be that all the assertions made about www.geonames.org/5128581 can be inferred to apply to http://dbpedia.org/resource/New_York_City and vice versa.

If DBpedia adds information about the year New York City was founded, as shown below:

http://dbpedia.org/resource/New_York_City1	dbpedia-owl:yearFounded	1624^^xsd:integer

One could automatically infer the following triple below:

http://www.geonames.org/5128581	dbpedia-owl:yearFounded	1624^^xsd:integer

While the property owl:sameAs provides a very powerful mechanism for mapping controlled vocabularies, it also entails its own risks. In some cases different institutions understand the extension (scope) of a resource differently, therefore adding or excluding different types of information. In this case, merging the two sets of information by using owl:sameAs can lead to logically inconsistent statements. Hence owl:sameAs should be used very carefully.

In the next section we will cover another mechanism for creating mappings between terms from two different controlled vocabularies in a more controlled manner, SPARQL.

SPARQL

SPARQL (SPARQL Protocol and RDF Query Language) is an RDF query language, like SQL is a query language for relational databases. It has multiple applications within the Semantic Web, including providing a mechanism to query multiple decentralized RDF repositories and being used to create inference rules. But in this section we will focus on SPARQL as the language to create mappings between terms from two controlled vocabularies in a controlled manner. Concretely, we will focus on the SPARQL CONSTRUCT query form.

SPARQL CONSTRUCT is one of the statements available in the SPARQL query language that returns a new RDF graph containing all the triples from the query solution. In a nutshell, this allows the creation of new assertions—triples—about a given resource.

In the context of creating mappings between two controlled vocabularies, SPARQL CONSTRUCT can be used to specify which triples from concept A in vocabulary A' will be integrated into its equivalent concept B in vocabulary B'.

Let's assume that DBpedia stores the year in which New York City was founded and who was the first mayor using the triples below:

http://dbpedia.org/resource/New_York_City	dbpedia-owl:yearFounded	1624^^xsd:integer
http://dbpedia.org/resource/New_York_City	dbpedia-owl:firstMayor	"Thomas Willett"@en

To create a mapping between the New York City from DBpedia and the New York City from Geonames by adding to Geonames only the information about the year it was founded, use the SPARQL CONSTRUCT statement below:

PREFIX dbpedia:<http://dbpedia.org/resource/>

PREFIX geonames:<http://www.geonames.org/>

CONSTRUCT {<http://www.geonames.org/5128581> geonames:yearFounded ?o}

WHERE { <http://dbpedia.org/resource/New_York_City> dbpedia:yearFounded ?o }

This statement will return an RDF graph (set of RDF statements) containing the information about the year in which New York City was founded, attached to the term from the Geonames controlled vocabulary as below:

http://www.geonames.org/5128581	geonames:yearFounded	1624^^xsd:integer

But it will avoid adding the information about who was its first mayor. Consequently, SPARQL CONSTRUCT is a powerful mechanism that provides a very flexible way to control what information gets integrated when creating mappings across terms from different controlled vocabularies.

VALUE VOCABULARIES

Two principal RDF vocabularies have been adopted in the Semantic Web community for representing bibliographic data.[11] On the one hand, Dublin

```
<info:doi/10.1134/S0003683806040089> a bibo:Article ;

dc:title "Effect of argillaceous minerals on the growth of phosphate-mobilizing
bacteria Bacillus subtilis"@en ;

        dc:date "2006-01-01" ;

        dc:isPartOf <urn:issn:23346587> ;

        bibo:volume "42" ;

        bibo:issue "4" ;

        bibo:pageStart "388" ;

        bibo:pageEnd "391" ;

        dc:creator <http://examples.net/contributors/2> ;


dc:creator <http://examples.net/contributors/1> ;

        bibo:authorList ( <http://examples.net/contributors/2> <http://examples.
net/contributors/1>) .


<urn:issn:23346587> a bibo:Journal ;

        dc:title "Applied Biochemistry and Microbiology"@en ;

        bibo:shortTitle "App Biochem and Biol"@en .
```

Figure 4.4 | **Linked data cloud example**

Core Metadata Initiative (DCMI) Metadata Terms (http://dublincore.org/
documents/dcmi-terms/) is present in around 70 percent of the datasets available
in the linked data cloud. On the other hand, the Bibliographic Ontology Specification (http://bibliontology.com) provides main concepts and properties for
describing citations and bibliographic references (i.e., quotes, books, articles, etc.).

These two vocabularies are complementary and elements from them often
appear together in the linked data cloud as in the example in figure 4.4.

VOCABULARY AND MODEL SELECTION

A critical step in integrating a vocabulary resource that can be used to enable
linking between multiple resources is to select the correct vocabulary. The
selection process should use a holistic approach that takes into account the
domain of the content, the amount of effort that your organization can put

into customization, the technology that will be using the vocabulary, and the long-term sustainability of the resource.

The first criterion in vocabulary selection is to make certain that the vocabulary fits the domain and subject matter of the content collections and data you are attempting to link. The next criterion is to assess the use case—and future potential use cases—to make certain that the vocabulary will be able to support it. A feature of the vocabulary that will likely need to be checked is its granularity and specificity. For example, if the collection is a catalog of books and the use case centers around personalization and matching users to new titles based on their past reading habits, chances are a vocabulary with a high level of granularity would not be necessary and broad topics would be sufficient. Likewise, if your domain dealt with clinical sciences and research communications, and the use case involved helping a service provider find a precise answer to a specific question, a vocabulary would probably need to be very granular in areas such as anatomy, drug names, and diseases and conditions.

The next step in selecting an appropriate vocabulary is to assess the actual content and quality of the vocabulary. This evaluation process is similar to traditional library roles including collecting and assessing appropriate reference resources: Is the information accurate? Is the information current? Is the publisher of the information trustworthy? Is the language appropriate for the audience and this application?

Once the questions of content and quality are addressed, you can begin to research how the vocabulary is governed. Specifically, how often is the vocabulary updated and what types of changes are made? And how are customers and subscribers notified of those changes? It is also important to learn what formats the vocabulary can be delivered in and how much effort it will take to convert it into a format that can be integrated with the application you are designing. This includes learning how much effort it will take to customize the vocabulary to meet your needs. Common customizations include adding elements to concepts and adding synonyms to terms.

Another consideration is the sustainability of the vocabulary. Some quality vocabularies that are "available" on the Web were built to support single projects and are no longer being updated. In some cases, it is not clear who the owner is and it is uncertain how long the vocabulary will be available. It is worth knowing if the vocabulary's publisher is a stable organization and what their business model is. Another consideration is gauging how much effort and resources (i.e., people) it will take to maintain and tailor the vocabulary to support the application you are building.

LINKING AUTHOR IDENTIFIERS

Although linked data technologies have tremendously facilitated the linkage of entities from disparate data sources, some challenges remain. One of these challenges is linking author identifiers; for example, those used in library cataloging such as LCNAF and those used in publisher metadata such as ORCID and Scopus.

In order to tackle this problem an ISO Standard called International Standard Name Identifier (ISNI) was published in 2012. It assigns persistent unique 16-digit identifying numbers to contributors of content—for example, researchers, authors, musicians, actors, publishers—to the public identities of parties (the name by which a party is publicly known).

ISNI registration is done through the following steps:

1. The publisher submits names for assignment through a registration agency.
2. This registration agency works with the publisher to ensure the quality and completeness of the information. It is then sent on to an Assignment Agency.
3. The assignment agency assigns as many existing ISNIs to the names as it can and creates new ones as needed, using algorithms and business rules.
4. Finally, the assignment agency returns a file of names with ISNIs attached to them to the publisher.

During this process, the new ISNIs are linked to identifiers from other data sources that represent the same resource. As you can see this is a very labor-intensive process, but it shows potential to result in a high level of confidence in the linkage.

An example would be the ISNI for Tim Berners-Lee (http://isni.org/isni/0000000124514311) that is linked to its identifier from LCNAF (http://id.loc.gov/authorities/names/n099010609).

From an STM perspective, there are many new and exciting trends that can significantly change research communications. Many are technical changes that leverage much of what are considered traditional skills in the library community. Much of the change will also require cultural changes across organizations before we can realize an ecosystem that would allow for content to be marked up with approved linked data-style identifiers. First, there must be demand from content creators to want to mark up their content and data. That demand could come from a sincere desire to share results for the advancement of science. But more likely, there will need to be specific incentivization and motivation from various third parties. As stated earlier, it is becoming more common for funding agencies to mandate that data be made available for publicly funded research. There are few requirements or specifics about how data should be represented or how to make it available in such a way that it can be reused. Collecting this as linked data could offer a strong option. Publishers could also play a role in helping authors mark up their content to sync up with discipline-specific resources that are authoritative. Motivation might include a star rating scale similar to the one Berners-Lee proposed. However, this would require participation from other partners—societies, agencies, consortia, and other organizations that would be willing and able to take responsibility for the publishing, governance, and maintenance of lists, vocabularies, and other resources as linked data.

Aside from promoting research and expertise and making it available for others to leverage, marking up objects formally within content to make it identifiable is becoming more and more important in terms of the reproducibility of scientific research. According to Elizabeth Iorns, and co-founder and CEO of Science Exchange, "One of the most important principles of the scientific method is reproducibility, the ability to replicate an experimental result."[12]

Notes

1. Stebbins Michael, "Expanding Public Access to the Results of Federally Funded Research," *Office of Science and Technology* blog, February 22, 2013, www.whitehouse .gov/blog/2013/02/22/expanding-public-access-results-federally-funded-research.

2. Trans-NIH BioMedical Informatics Coordinating Committee, "NIH Data Sharing Policies," 2013, www.nlm.nih.gov/NIHbmic/nih_data_sharing_policies.html.

3. T. Bloom, E. Ganley, and M. Winker, "Data Access for the Open Access Literature: PLOS's Data Policy," *PLOS Biology* 12, no. 2 (2014), doi: 10.1371/journal.pbio.1001797, http://journals.plos.org/plosbiology/article?id=10.1371/journal.pbi0.1001797; Wellcome Trust, 2010, "Policy on Data Management and Sharing," http://www .wellcome.ac.uk/About-us/Policy/Policy-and-positionstatements/WTX035043.htm.

4. C. G. Begley, and L. M. Ellis, "Drug Development: Raise Standards for Preclinical Cancer Research," *Nature* 483 (2012): 531–33, doi: 10.1038/483531a, www.nature.com/ nature/journal/v483/n7391/full/483531a.html.

5. Florian Prinz, Thomas Schlange, and Khusru Asadullah, 2011, "Believe It or Not: How Much Can We Rely on Published Data on Potential Drug Targets?" Nature Reviews

Drug Discovery, doi:10.1038/nrd3439-c1, www.nature.com/nrd/journal/v10/n9/full/nrd3439-c1.html.

6. N. A. Vasilevsky, M. H. Brush, H. Paddock, L. Ponting, S. J. Tripathy, G. M. LaRocca, and M. A. Haendel, "On the Reproducibility of Science: Unique Identification of Research Resources in the Biomedical Literature," *Peer Journal* 1 (2013): e148, https://peerj.com/articles/148/.

7. Michael Lauruhn and Véronique Malaisé, "Elsevier Metadata Design for Smart Content," presented at DCMI Science & Metadata Community Workshop, 2011, http://wiki.dublincore.org/images/5/58/Elsevier_DC-SAMv3.pdf.

8. Eric Miller, Uche Ogbuji, Victoria Mueller, and Kathy MacDougall, "Bibliographic Framework as a Web of Data: Linked Data Model and Supporting Services," November 11, 2012, www.loc.gov/bibframe/pdf/marcld-report-11–21–2012.pdf.

9. Corey A. Harper and Barbara B. Tillett, "Library of Congress Controlled Vocabularies and Their Application to the Semantic Web," *Cataloging & Classification Quarterly* 43, nos. 3/4 (2007): 47–68.

10. "AGROVOC," *Wikipedia: The Free Encyclopedia*, Wikimedia Foundation, December 29, 2015, http://en.wikipedia.org/wiki/AGROVOC.

11. Food and Agriculture Organization of the United Nations (FAO), "AGROVOC Linked Open Data," http://aims.fao.org/standards/agrovoc/linked-open-data; www.w3.org/2005/Incubator/lld/XGR-lld-vocabdataset-20111025/#Value_vocabularies.

12. "About," Validation by Science Exchange, http://validation.scienceexchange.com/#/about.

A DIVISION OF LABOR

The Role of Schema.org in a Semantic Web Model of Library Resources

Carol Jean Godby

LIBRARY METADATA AS LINKED DATA

This chapter describes some of OCLC's experiments with Schema.org as the foundation for a linked data model of library resources. The most important reason for giving Schema.org serious consideration is that this is the vocabulary endorsed by the world's major search engines at a time when a user's quest for information is more likely to begin on the broader Web than in a library or even a library website.[1] But there is a simpler and more pragmatic reason for taking a serious look at Schema.org. At a time of unprecedented uncertainty, Schema.org offers the promise that at least some of the effort involved in designing the next-generation standards for library data can be undertaken by a trusted third party. As a general-purpose vocabulary that is compliant with linked data principles, Schema.org addresses the requirements expressed in the Library of Congress publication *On the Record* for a solution that recognizes the Web as a technology platform and as a means for the discovery and delivery of resources that fulfill a user's information request.[2]

Yet many standards experts view the Schema.org vocabulary as too superficial and narrowly focused on the commercial sector to serve the needs of libraries. Some researchers at OCLC were among the initial skeptics. We noted, for example, that the "schema:CreativeWork," represented as an RDF class, would form the core of a Semantic Web model of the contents of a library collection. But a reasonable first impression is that this term offers little to a sophisticated discussion. The definition appears simplistic— "The most generic kind of creative work, including books, movies, photographs, software programs, etc." —and it is accompanied by a flat list of attributes, or RDF properties, such as "schema:author," "schema:isbn," "schema:publisher," and "schema:about," which could be used to assemble a set of statements resembling a primitive Dublin Core record.[3] Yet an accumulating body of model fragments and other experimental results is starting to show that Schema.org is actually rich enough to keep pace with mature thinking about the replacement for MARC and other standards that aim to modernize the data architecture for the library community. This chapter recounts the highlights of the experiments conducted at OCLC by focusing on three works: a published memoir, a children's fairy tale, and a recorded multimedia performance. It summarizes some of the arguments presented in the book *Library Linked Data in the Cloud.*[4] But the perspective given here is more personal, is focused more directly on the arguments in favor of data models featuring Schema.org, and is closer to the leading edge of our analysis.

THE FIRST MATURE MODEL OF BIBLIOGRAPHIC RESOURCES AND A REFORMULATION IN SCHEMA.ORG

In the months before Schema.org was published in the summer of 2011, linked data research at OCLC was focused on the task of expressing the contents of MARC records as a network of RDF statements. In the preceding years, OCLC researchers had contributed to the development of Semantic Web standards, worked in multiple venues with the international community of library standards experts to shape the argument that the linked data paradigm was consistent with the values of librarianship, and published the first linked data versions of VIAF, FAST, and the Dewey Decimal Classification.[5] Attention had been initially directed to the task of converting library authority files to RDF, not only at OCLC but also in the broader library community in the United States and Europe. This focus made sense. Authority files were about people, places, organizations, and concepts, and were consistent with the linked data directive to create descriptions of persistent objects in the real world.[6] From a technical perspective, the contents of library authority files were already normalized, and the underlying semantics of the MARC authority record could map relatively easily into first-generation Semantic Web standards such as the Simple Knowledge Organization System, or SKOS.[7] In 2008, researchers affiliated with the Library of Congress published a seminal study that produced a linked data representation of the Library of Congress subject and name authority files, paving the way for the development of http://id.loc.gov, one of the most widely accessed RDF datasets published in the library community.[8]

However, the description of creative works, or bibliographic resources, was identified as a more challenging task and a top priority for future work. This was the conclusion of the Library Linked Data Incubator Group, an international committee of library standards experts convened by the World Wide Web Consortium.[9] Bibliographic description is problematic because library standards are large, semantically complex, and designed primarily for human readers, not machine processes. But just as the *Library Linked Data Incubator Group Final Report* was being finalized, the British Library published a data model and the first large-scale proof of concept that bibliographic records that support a sophisticated use case for a major national library could be decomposed into networks of RDF statements. The result was a dataset representing approximately three million holdings in the British National Bibliography. A high-level view of the model would become an iconic diagram. Details of the model were later described in a series of tutorials by Dodds.[10]

The design of the British Library Data Model is conceptually simple and has been widely replicated, despite the deceptively cluttered appearance of the model diagram. At the center of the model is a "bibliographic resource" defined in the Bibliographic Ontology, which may either be realized as a self-contained work or a member of a series.[11] The resource came into being through a "publication event," which defines relationships between the bibliographic resource and a set of people and organizations acting in a particular time and place. The creator or "author," can be a person, who has a name and a birth date; or an organization, which has a name and an address. Finally, the bibliographic resource may have a "subject" defined from the various kinds of things that populate traditional library authority files—that is, people, places, and concepts.

The model is expressed as RDF instance data containing persistent identifiers for people, places, organizations, and concepts, supplemented by publisher-maintained resource identifiers such as ISBNs or ISSNs. Relationships are expressed primarily by concepts defined by Dublin Core Terms, such as "dct:subject," "dct:contributor," and "dct:isPartOf." Other features of the model are described by a vocabulary maintained by the British Library and supplemented with twelve other sources of terminology: standards endorsed by the W3C, RDF vocabularies published by the library community such as Dublin Core and VIAF, and ontologies developed by other researchers interested in the intersection of the Semantic Web and language, linguistics, and references to written works, such as de Melo.[12]

When it was first published, the British Library Data Model represented a major advance over previous Semantic Web models of resources managed by libraries, both conceptually and technically. Conceptually, the model succeeds at reducing the complexity of library standards for bibliographic description to a few simple building blocks that represent the most important real-world objects and their relationships to resources managed by libraries—people who are creators or contributors; organizations that publish or distribute; people, places, or topics that the resources are about; and so on. In addition, the model is described in accordance with conventions established in the linked data paradigm. Thus it uses published vocabularies wherever possible; it refers to as many entities as possible with URIs from published RDF datasets; and it minimizes literal text strings while maximizing cross-linking. Technically, the model exhibits attention to the details of the linked data architecture, such as the specification of persistent URI patterns for every entity defined in the model. To encourage consumption, the outputs of the British Library experiment are available from a mature website with institutional branding, where data consumers can download the entire dataset or view descriptions in RDF/XML, JSON, RDF/Turtle, and a human-readable format.[13]

A FIRST DRAFT OF THE OCLC MODEL OF BIBLIOGRAPHIC DESCRIPTION

Also in 2011, as researchers were evaluating the British Library Data Model as a possible foundation for OCLC's model of linked bibliographic data, Schema .org was published. Like many other modeling experts, they initially wondered whether Schema.org supported rather than undermined the linked data paradigm because the Schema.org vocabulary appeared to be shallow and permitted the use of text strings where URIs would have been more appropriate. Though a commitment to linked data appeared to be optional, the first announcement assured Semantic Web advocates that Schema.org indeed supported RDFa encodings.[14] Additional investigation revealed that the chief data architect for Schema.org was R. V. Guha, who has a long history of involvement in knowledge engineering research and the development of Semantic Web standards, including RDF Schema.[15]

OCLC researchers were also skeptical of Schema.org because the vocabulary seemed too focused on commercial products, which overlap only partially with the curatorial needs of libraries. But a quick test revealed that Schema .org offered nearly the same coverage as the fourteen vocabularies used in the British Library Data Model. These equivalences are illustrated in figure 5.1, which represent comparable descriptions of a memoir described in WorldCat at www.worldcat.org/title/memoir-my-life-and-themes/oclc/43477327 and in the British Library dataset at http://bnb.data.bl.uk/doc/resource/008140605. To highlight the commonalities, the descriptions contain text strings, not URIs. In the real instance data, of course, all RDF predicates except string literals such as titles and dates are expressed as URIs that conform to the patterns suggested by figure 5.1 in the British Library data and derived primarily from FAST, VIAF, and LCSH in the OCLC data. The small number of gaps, such as the British Library model of the statement of responsibility as an event, would be addressed by an extension vocabulary for Schema.org proposed by OCLC, a topic discussed in more detail below.

BRITISH LIBRARY DATA MODEL	OCLC MODEL
a bibo:BibliographicResource;	a schema:Book;
dc:title "Memoir : my life and themes";	schema:name "Memoir : my life and themes";
dcterms:creator "Conor Cruise O'Brien";	schema:author "Conor Cruise O'Brien";
blterms:datePublished "1999";	schema:datePublished "1999";
blterms:publication <event>;	schema:publisher "Profile";
dcterms:language "English";	schema:inLanguage "English";
dcterms:subject "Statesmen";	schema:about "Diplomats";
bibo:isbn10 "1861971516";	schema:isbn "1861971516";
isbd:01953 "470 p.";	schema:numberOfPages "470 p.";
dcterms:description :"includes index";	schema:description :"includes index";
dcterms:spatial "Ireland".	schema:place "Ireland".

Figure 5.1 | **Two Descriptions of a Memoir in the British National Bibliography**

In short, a reformulation using Schema.org vocabulary appeared to be simpler without significant loss of expressiveness. Because the description is formulated from terms defined in a single namespace, the concept space is clearly specified. But the British Library solution raises questions. Is "dcterms:accrualPeriodicity" in or out of scope? Does the presence of the BIBO definition of 'ISBN' preclude the use of the DC-Terms solution for describing ISBNs? Is an "foaf:Document" the same thing as a "bibo:BibliographicResource," and if so, is the property "foaf:topic" equivalent to "dcterms:subject" because both assert an "aboutness" relationship between a resource and a real-world object? Are these equivalences formally expressed in the model, or are they informally assumed? Technically, a small set of namespaces also means that instance data is easier to produce and maintain. In addition, the simpler solution has a greater chance of widespread adoption because prospective advocates do not have to engage in the task of vetting each vocabulary and substituting other choices that are more appropriate or timely. But in one important respect, the vocabulary choices for encoding instance data are a side issue because the most important details of the underlying high-level model can be preserved in the transformation. Thus a description encoded with Schema.org vocabulary is still centered on a creative work, with properties that identify the people, places, organizations, and concepts that brought it into being and define a context for interpreting it.

Arguments about conceptual simplicity and scope of coverage can be stated without considering the stature of Schema.org as a de facto standard, but the case is stronger when this fact is acknowledged. Right after Schema.org was announced, bloggers pointed out that the new ontology might curtail some of the experiments with vocabulary development made visible by projects such as the British Library Data Model. Nevertheless, the declaration of a shareable semantics from a group of influential organizations with a commercial incentive could only be interpreted as a positive development for the Semantic Web.[16] In a recent presentation, Guha argued that the major Internet search engines have long been interested in structured data, but have been unable to solicit enough high-quality input from data providers.[17] Schema.org is the latest incentive, and as in earlier solutions such as the HTML <meta> tag or microdata, the promised return is a Rich Snippet, a Knowledge Card, and generally greater visibility in the marketplace where most users now begin their quest for information.[18]

The Schema.org vocabulary is designed to strike a balance between simplicity and sophistication, making it easy for webmasters to say simple things, while providing a platform for data managers representing specialized communities of practice to say complex things, to paraphrase a point made by Guha in his 2014 presentation. Proposals for enhancement are managed by community groups sponsored by the W3C, following a pattern established by other web standards initiatives such as Dublin Core, SKOS, and RDF. As Schema.org evolves, the vocabulary is enriched with ontologies developed by third parties, some of whose interests align with those of libraries. For example, Good-Relations defines an ontology for e-commerce and has recently been integrated with Schema.org.[19] Some of the vocabulary defined in GoodRelations being evaluated by librarians as a model for library holdings is more easily consumed by machine processes and more readily understood by the major search engines than the text-heavy standards used in the library community.[20]

PUBLISHING AND EXTENDING SCHEMA.ORG

In 2012 OCLC published the first draft of a linked data model for biblio-graphic description expressed in Schema.org as RDFa markup on approxi-mately 300 million MARC catalog records accessible from WorldCat.org.[21] These descriptions were built upon previous successes with linked data models of library authority files, featuring URIs from RDF datasets representing the Dewey Decimal Classification, the Library of Congress Subject Headings, the Library of Congress Name Authority File, VIAF, and FAST. The outcome was the largest set of linked bibliographic data on the Web by many orders of magnitude, and a proof-of-concept demonstration of linked data as a viable next-generation data architecture for library resource description. The World-Cat linked data was updated in 2014 with URIs from the recently published WorldCat Works dataset, which uses the latest generation of FRBR-inspired clustering algorithms to group bibliographic records with similar content.[22]

The demonstration has a technical as well as an ontological component. Technically, the result demonstrates that the technology stack, which fea-tured map-reduce jobs implemented on Hadoop clusters and Semantic Web development tools such as those described in the compilation maintained by the World Wide Web Consortium, could handle the sheer magnitude of a data-processing task that produces tens of billions of RDF triples and ren-ders them searchable in real time.[23] Once mature, the processes could refresh the markup on WorldCat records in a matter of hours, not days, producing BIBFRAME instead of Schema.org encodings in a late processing step when this result was requested in a joint experiment with the Library of Congress in early 2013. Conceptually, even the first experiment demonstrated that a simple entity-relationship model expressed in Schema.org could capture assertions about every resource type described in the WorldCat catalog data. In fact, the Schema.org definitions of "Person," "Organization," "Creative Work," "Place," and "Topic" appeared to be robust enough to serve as the real-world referents for the URIs defined in the linked data versions of VIAF and FAST, which were republished in 2014. In these revisions, a VIAF or FAST "Person" such as Peter Tchaikovsky is defined as a "schema:Person," matching the RDF assertions about the Russian composer published in the bibliographic descriptions accessible from WorldCat.org.

EXTENSION VOCABULARIES

A more detailed examination of the descriptions generated from the OCLC experiments is deferred to the next section, but even a cursory look at Schema .org reveals gaps that need to be filled to keep pace with linked data experiments being conducted elsewhere in the library community. For example, figure 5.1 shows that the Schema.org description that could be generated in 2011 was slightly less expressive than the corresponding British Library Data Model description because of missing or imprecise terms that should be synonymous with "dcterms:isPartOf" and "dcterms:spatial." But such problems are now being addressed. In 2012 OCLC founded the W3C-sponsored Schema Bib Extend Community Group, which includes librarians, publishers, and integrated library system (or ILS) vendors who share OCLC's perspective regarding the importance of Schema.org in the conversion of legacy bibliographic descriptions to linked data.[24]

As at OCLC, the Schema Bib Extend group begins a modeling exercise by selecting a problem in library resource description and handcrafting a set of statements using terms defined in Schema.org. The analysis demonstrates what Schema.org successfully covers, but it also reveals gaps, inconsistencies, or terms that are incorrectly placed in the ontology. Possible amendments to Schema.org are discussed on W3C-managed mailing lists such as "public-schemabibex" or "public-vocabs," some of which advance to the status of a formal recommendation to the managers of Schema.org.[25] In October 2014 Schema.org adopted the recommendations from the Schema Bib Extend group for "schema:hasPart" and schema "isPartOf." Schema.org has also adopted the refinements of the structured parts of a journal citation recommended by the Bib Extend group for the property "schema:issueNumber" on "schema:PublicationIssue" and for "schema:volumeNumber" on "schema:PublicationVolume." In addition, Schema.org now contains the "schema:CreativeWork" properties "schema:workExample" and "schema:exampleOfWork," which emerged from OCLC's experiments with the implementation of Work-to-Work relationships concepts defined in FRBR and RDA. The use of these relationships is discussed later in this chapter.

In the absence of a comprehensive standard, however, model development requires a proving ground for experimenting with candidate vocabulary even before it has been submitted for public review. To meet this need, OCLC introduced the BiblioGraph.net extension vocabulary in 2014, which has the look and feel of Schema.org because it has been constructed from a common code base. One outcome is a visualization of the impact of proposed extensions on the Schema.org vocabulary. For example, "Agent" can be defined as an extension of "schema:Thing" and has "schema:Person" and "schema:Organization" as subclasses, borrowing the definition created in the Friend of a Friend (or FOAF) ontology. According to the FOAF documentation, "Agent" is "useful in a few places . . . where 'Person' would have been overly specific."[26] In effect, the BiblioGraph definition acts as a technical "pass-through" from FOAF to Schema.org that shows how terms defined in an external vocabulary could be positioned in an ontology that can be directly consumed by general-purpose search engines. In BiblioGraph, the "Agent" class has been proposed as a useful place to define properties such as "bgn:publishedBy" and "bgn:translator," both because people and organizations can have these relationships to creative works and because it is not always possible to distinguish between them in MARC records or other bibliographic descriptions. BiblioGraph and the informally named "cherry-picking" approach observable in the British Library Data Model may have superficial similarities, but there is one important difference. While both efforts aim to expand the scope of Semantic Web vocabularies to advance the development of resource descriptions that can support services offered by libraries, a solution built on Schema.org has the equally important goal of extending the boundary of a shared semantics. And the outcome is a single ontology that is explicitly specified, comprehensible to human readers, and actionable by machine processes.

Thus the models developed at OCLC emerge from the assumption that many concepts already defined in Schema.org are essentially the same as those defined by library standards experts, including top-level classes such as "schema:Thing," "schema:Person," "schema:Organization," "schema:Topic," and "schema:Place." In fact, most properties defined for "schema:CreativeWork" have such shareable semantics, such as "author," "director," "publisher," "ISBN," "genre," "copyrightYear," and "audience." With an extension vocabulary such as BiblioGraph, OCLC provides a forum for representing other concepts defined by the library community that are also understandable and useful outside the narrow community of professional catalogers. For example, Schema.org is especially deficient in the inventory of relationships among creative works, as well as formats and resource types, such as "microform," which is defined in

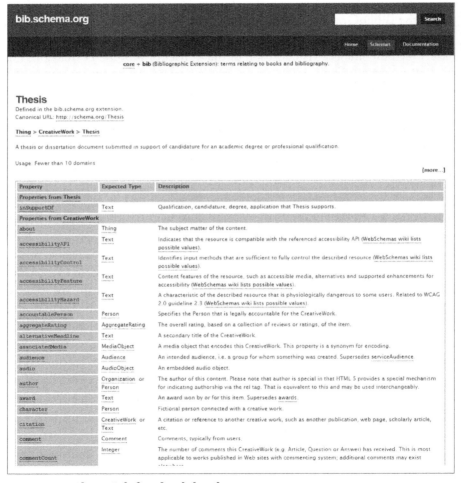

Figure 5.2 | **"Thesis" defined in bib.schema.org**

BiblioGraph as a subclass of "schema:Product" because it is a physical object that can be bought and sold. The expertise of library standards experts is especially strong on these topics, of course, and OCLC's modeling experts believe that definitions of translations, adaptations, product forms, and other derivatives that could result from their engagement with Schema.org are likely to be useful to other professional managers of bibliographic resources and many information seekers.[27]

Much of BiblioGraph.net has recently been absorbed experimentally into Schema.org as a more closely integrated "reviewed/hosted Extension."[28] Reviewed extensions are also interpreted as an overlay on the core Schema vocabulary, to which subclasses and properties would typically be added. An example is shown in figure 5.2. Here, "bib:Thesis" is defined as a subclass of "schema:Creative" and inherits all of its properties, such as "schema:name," "schema:about," "schema:author," and so on. This core description is enhanced with the additional property "bib:inSupportOf," which applies only to a thesis and describes the academic purpose for which it was produced. Extension vocabularies such as bib.schema.org are formally recognized only if they are maintained by a recognized community of practice such as the Schema Bib Extend community group. Other extensions are being discussed for the domain of library resource management, and for communities of practice elsewhere on the Web.

TOWARD A MODELING DIVISION OF LABOR

The "reviewed extension" proposed by the Schema.org editors presents the opportunity for librarians and other communities of practice to engage more closely with an important target audience, eliminating some of the guesswork about whether domain-specific vocabularies are visible to general-purpose search engines. Other communities are confronting the same issue. For example, a person suffering from hives might issue a Google search for advice on treatment, which returns a Knowledge Card, and associates the condition with the medical term "urticaria."

The user's query is more likely to yield rich results if authoritative health care sites are published with structured descriptions that bridge the gap between the frames of reference of the general population and the professional. For both the medical and library communities, it is possible to imagine a model in which a broadly understandable vocabulary is defined in Schema.org, while a more complete description is modeled with terminology defined with the greater precision required by researchers, practitioners, and other specialists.

By designing such a model, data architects acknowledge the utility of the "linguistic division of labor" made famous by the philosopher of language Hilary Putnam.[29] His work addresses a classic question: does the meaning of a word reside only inside a person's head, or is it in the public sphere? Difficulties ensue if the answer is the first choice. It would be impossible, for example, to verify that the tasteless, odorless clear liquid that sustains life called "water" by one community is the same substance assigned the chemical structure H_2O by chemists, and is different from the embalming fluid called "water" in some drug subcultures. But as Putnam argues, if the meaning of "water" is instead a social construct, it can be built up by communities that have different interests, levels of expertise, and requirements for scientific truth who cooperate through a network of trust. Thus most of us in the lay public have no practical need for knowing the chemical structure of water, but we sometimes have to rely on experts to vouch for the fact that the clear liquid in our drinking glasses is life-giving and not poisonous. The conception of word meaning as a social construct is still relevant today, and is at the heart of the theory of reference defined by the Semantic Web. Linked data principles identify the primacy of real-world objects, and conventions such as "Cool URIs" interpret the Web as a corpus of facts about these objects, which require collaborative effort and a range of expertise to arrive at the truth.[30]

But it remains to be determined how the division of labor should be implemented in the design of library linked data. In the work under way at OCLC, community input would be solicited to distinguish between the terms that would be formally proposed as candidates for inclusion in Schema.org, and the vocabulary that would be maintained in BiblioGraph or bib.schema.org, which defines the high-level concepts in the domain of library resources and the transactions that involve them. This distinction is a proxy for the differences in the language of the public and that of experts, and it serves two use cases. The first supports discovery through general-purpose search engines, and the second is required for long-term curation and other functions of libraries that enable the fulfillment of the user's information request.

The same distinction emerges from our joint analysis with the BIBFRAME team at the Library of Congress.[31] But many details remain to be specified. For example, the vocabulary of experts will likely be much larger and more complex than the stub defined in BiblioGraph. Perhaps most of it will never be directly consumable by search engines, except for high-level concepts that comprise a metalanguage of sorts that could be exposed through the pathway we have defined. For example, the properties defined for "schema:MedicalCondition" include "treatment," "risk factor," "cause," "pathophysiology," and "prevention," whose expected values are text strings or URIs defined in specialized vocabularies, some of which are maintained by the library community. Conversely, the vocabulary that can be exposed through a general-purpose ontology such as Schema.org and the BiblioGraph extension may be larger than is acknowledged in MARC or other library standards. This is the working hypothesis of much of the linked data work now being conducted at OCLC, as we argued in Godby, Wang, and Mixter and in the examples in the next section of this chapter.[32] For example, BiblioGraph defines "translator" and "translation of work," but so does RDA.[33] By defining these terms in BiblioGraph, we are claiming they exist in the language of the general public, which makes them candidates for eventual absorption into Schema.org. The same observation motivates the work to produce "unconstraine" definitions of all RDA relationships, which reduce to commonsense definitions with no dependency on the ontological claims of FRBR.[34] In other words, "translation" is like "water." Many users probably consider its definition to be clear enough, so they don't need to understand its chemical structure, as long as a recognized community of trusted experts does.

MODELING BEYOND PUBLISHED MONOGRAPHS

A focus on the relatively well-understood descriptions of published monographs such as the excerpt shown in figure 5.1 makes it easy to underestimate the true scope of the job required to transform the data architecture for library resource description. Unfortunately, the change will not happen completely through a simple record-by-record mapping from MARC to the new format. The transformation also requires the development of an entity-relationship model with ever-increasing granularity and algorithms that can discover evidence for the model in existing data. But when the algorithms reach their inevitable upper limits, it will be necessary to design a more aspirational model that is populated with human guidance by enacting recommendations for future descriptive practice. Though the larger set of tasks is challenging and multidimensional, OCLC's experiments make us confident that the Schema.org ontology can evolve with the demands that will have to be put on it.

A FAIRY TALE

An informal progress report on OCLC's approach to the modeling of linked bibliographic data can be assembled by examining two MARC records accessible from WorldCat.org. The first is a description of *The Nutcracker and the Mouse King*, a fairy tale written by the nineteenth-century German author E. T. A. Hoffmann and translated into English by Joachim Neugroschel. The second record describes a movie that captures a live performance of Tchaikovsky's ballet *The Nutcracker* at the Bolshoi Theatre in Moscow in 1989. The ballet is based on Hoffmann's tale.

Figure 5.3 shows critical details of the MARC record describing *The Tale of the Nutcracker*. The 041, 240, 245, 500, 700, and 740 fields reveal the relationships between the English derivative and a German original. The 041 field specifies the language of the cataloged work as English and the language of the original as German. The title of the cataloged work is listed in the 245 field; and the title of the original German work is listed in the 240, or "Uniform Title" field, which is prescribed by cataloging rules "when a work has appeared under varying titles, necessitating that a particular title be chosen to represent the work."[35] E. T. A. Hoffman is listed as the author of the English translation, perhaps because the cataloged work is identified as a variant of the original. The 500 field identifies the translator as Joachim Neugroschel, and the 245 $c lists a relationship between Hoffmann's work and *The Tale of the Nutcracker*, which has an unspecified link to Alexander Dumas. A list of 700 fields associate Hoffmann, Neugroschel, and Dumas with entries in the Library of Congress Name Authority file and the Dumas work is listed in the 740 field as an uncontrolled related title.

In sum, the MARC record excerpted in figure 5.3 describes a complex network of Agent-to-Work and Work-to-Work relationships. But not every detail is algorithmically recoverable. The details of the model that can be populated automatically by mapping from the semantics of the MARC record are captured in the RDFa markup, which is accessible from a tab labeled "Linked Data" at the bottom of the page in the associated WorldCat.org display. Figure 5.4 is a graphical representation of the most important details. The entities, or classes, are shown as white boxes; relationships, or properties, are shown as labeled arrows; and literals, such as "2007," are shown as floating strings. The names of the entities—"Person," "Creative Work," "Organization," and "Topic"—as well as the names of the relationships, displayed in italics, are imported from the corresponding RDF markup.

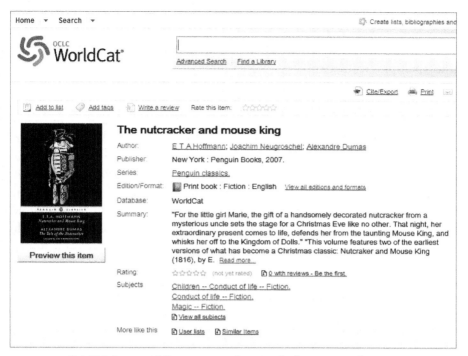

Figure 5.3 | **A MARC record for a 2007 edition of *The Nutcracker and the Mouse King*, WorldCat ID # '76967162'**

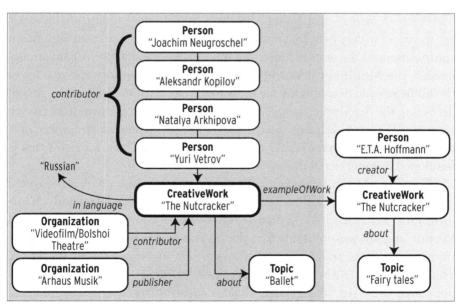

Figure 5.4 | **Entities and relationships revealed in the RDF statements for *The Nutcracker and the Mouse King***

As figure 5.4 implies, the RDF representation of the MARC record identifies multiple creative works connected through a translation relationship. The properties associating the Creative Work with other entities form machine-understandable RDF statements that correctly assert that "E. T. A. Hoffmann is the author of the creative work with the title *Nussknacker and Mausekönig*," "E. T. A. Hoffmann is the author of the creative work with the title *The Nutcracker and the Mouse King*," "The creative work with the title *The Nutcracker and the Mouse King* is published by an Organization with the name Penguin Books," which has a publication date of 2007 and is about Magic. But the RDF representation identifies Joachim Neugroschel only as a "contributor," not as a "translator," because the MARC-to-RDF conversion algorithms do not parse the free text in the MARC 500 field or other notes. For a similar reason, the RDF does not encode precise details about the Alexander Dumas version of *The Nutcracker* because the MARC record does not contain machine-understandable encodings of the relationship, perhaps because it is not clear even from the human-readable text.

The MARC and corresponding RDF descriptions of *The Nutcracker and the Mouse King* point to two areas of research in OCLC's next-generation models of bibliographic description. First, the Multilingual WorldCat project recognizes that nearly two thirds of WorldCat catalog records now represent non-English works—works that have the most complex publication histories, are the most widely held by libraries, represent arguably the most significant contributions to the world's literary canon, and are the most commonly translated.[36] The Multilingual WorldCat project aims to improve the quality of the bibliographic descriptions for these materials, with the long-term goal of delivering the description as well as a copy of the work in the searcher's chosen language. Though linked data is a means to this end, incremental improvements can made to the source MARC records as a useful side effect, a point that is developed in more detail in Smith-Yoshimura and Godby.[37]

For example, the important entities and relationships can be discovered more easily if the 041 field names the source and target languages and a "Uniform Title" field identifies the translation source. In addition, the Multilingual WorldCat team recommends that the description contain the name of the translator and the translation relationship in a machine-processable form. Thus if the 700 field for "Joachim Neugroschel" had contained $4 subfield populated with "trn," the MARC Relator code for "translator," the "schema: contributor" property could have been promoted to the more specific value, "bgn:translator."[38] This is a minor shortcoming in an otherwise high-quality record—which, unsurprisingly, is easily transformed into a set of expressive RDF statements.

The second area of research can be inferred from implicit references to the concepts defined in the FRBR Group I model.[39] A bibliographic record accessible from a library catalog or an aggregation such as WorldCat.org typically describes a Manifestation; a translation is an Expression of a Work; and an Item must be delivered to fulfill the information request that originated in the catalog. The linked data descriptions now available as RDFa markup on WorldCat catalog records build on nearly fifteen years of research conducted at OCLC on the problem of algorithmically discovering FRBR concepts in collections of MARC records.[40] Three conclusions emerge from this research. First, it is still necessary to distinguish among Work, Expression, Manifestation, and Item because these concepts are motivated by the user's need to find, identify, select, and obtain resources that satisfy his or her request for information, regardless of whether the search begins in a library catalog or on the Web. Second, the essential distinctions defined by FRBR and RDA elaborations can be captured using the properties defined for "schema:CreativeWork" and some commonsense extensions defined in BiblioGraph or other vocabularies maintained by library standards experts. The main problem is that Schema.org needs to be enhanced with richer content-to-content and agent-to-content relations. Finally, and more narrowly, the model of translations developed by the Multilingual WorldCat project can be viewed as a prototype for defining other content-to-content relations.

A rough draft of the solution is already visible in the high-level view shown in figure 5.4. On the left side, against the orange background, is a description based on the definition of the FRBR Manifestation, which describes a volume that was published by Penguin Books in 2007. On the right side, against the green background, is a more abstract description based on the definition of the FRBR Work. The Manifestation description is derived from a single MARC record, but the Work description is automatically generated from a set of similar MARC records and published as an entry with a persistent URI in the WorldCat Works dataset.

The clustering process is described in more detail in Godby, Wang, and Mixter, but it is conceptually simple.[41] The first step produces a group of records whose MARC 1xx "author" and 245 "title" fields match in a string comparison. A subsequent step considers information extracted from the corresponding VIAF descriptions for the authors, which contains lists of their published monographs in multiple languages and has the effect of pulling translations into the cluster. In the final step, a WorldCat Works description is constructed from the clustered records by extracting properties that describe the content, such as "schema:description," "schema:about," and "schema:genre"; as well as agents responsible for the content, such as "schema:contributor" and "schema:editor."

Important details of the Work and the Manifestation descriptions and the property that associates them is shown more explicitly in the RDF statements excerpted in figure 5.5. In literal terms, the object described when the URI <http://www.worldcat.org/title/nutcracker-and-mouse-king/oclc/76967162> is de-referenced—that is, the Penguin edition of the book *The Nutcracker and Mouse King*—is a product with a model number, or an ISBN. As a result, the Manifestation has class assignments of "schema:CreativeWork" and "schema: ProductModel." But since the "Work" described in the document accessible from the URI <http://worldcat.org/entity/work/id/839867> has no properties

---

<http:// http://www.worldcat.org/title/nutcracker-and-mouse-king/oclc/76967162>
    a schema:CreativeWork, schema:ProductModel
        schema:name "The nutcracker and mouse king";
        schema:exampleOfWork <http://worldcat.org/entity/work/id/839867>;
        schema:contributor "Neugroschel";
        schema:creator "ETA Hoffmann";
        schema:isbn "xxx";
        schema:publisher "Penguin Books";
        schema:publicationDate "2007";
        schema:about "Magic".

<http://worldcat.org/entity/work/id/839867>
    a schema:CreativeWork
        schema:name "Der Nussnacker...
        schema: creator "E.T.A Hoffmann;
        schema: description "After hearing how her toy nutcracker got his ugly face, a little girl helps break
        the spell and watches him change into a handsome prince."
        schema:about "Mice";

Figure 5.5 | **RDF/Turtle excerpts of Manifestation and Work descriptions for the 2007 Penguin edition of *The Nutcracker and Mouse King***

that allude to a physical presence, the single class assignment of "schema: CreativeWork" is sufficient. The property "schema:exampleOfWork" establishes that a semantic relationship exists between the Manifestation and the Work. But the above discussion implies that the 041 and 240 fields of the Manifestation description contain some of the detail required to assign the more specific property recently absorbed from Bibliograph.net, "schema:translationOfWork." Algorithms that exploit this information and operate on the entire corpus of translated resources accessible from WorldCat,org and VIAF are now being tested, and the newly published terms for translators and translations are beginning to appear in published RDF statements.

Though simple, this example has unexpected theoretical and practical implications for the implementation of FRBR as linked data. At a high level, this data illustrates the configuration shown in the right-hand panel of figure 5.6, which contrasts with the familiar diagram depicting hierarchical relationships among FRBR Works, Expressions, Manifestations, and Items shown on the left.[42] In other words, OCLC's linked data model of bibliographic description is simply a network of objects typed as "schema:CreativeWork," all accessible through persistent URIs, with no presumptive hierarchical relationships. If they form a cluster of related creative works, they are at least connected via the semantically null "exampleOfWork" relationship, which may be upgraded to the more meaningful "translationOfWork" if certain details are present.

One consequence of this design is that Expression as a class is remodeled as a set of relationships among creative works, such as "translation," "adaptation," and others defined in RDA Work-to-Work and Work-to-Expression ontologies.[43] Another consequence is that the need to partition a set of properties across a hierarchy is eliminated. In most implementations of FRBR and RDA, creators, titles, or subjects are assigned only to Works, while contributors, series titles, or publication details can be assigned only to Manifestations, and

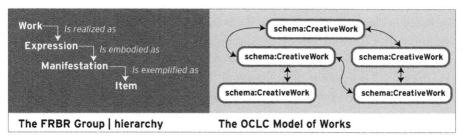

Figure 5.6 | **Hierarchical and graph models of creative works**

so on. Instead, the RDF statements reproduced in figure 5.5 show that Works and Manifestations both have subjects, titles, and authors, but only the Manifestation description has properties describing a publisher, page count, and other evidence of a physical presence. Likewise, an Item description would be assigned the Schema.org types "CreativeWork" and "IndividualProduct" if it contained a bar code. Thus, the hierarchical data models of FRBR and RDA have been replaced with a "trigger" model, which recognizes that most properties defined for the description of a creative work do not induce further ontological distinctions; only those that indicate physicality, uniqueness, or membership in a set of identical objects do. If present, these properties trigger the assignment of an additional Schema.org type.

A BALLET

With this background, it is now possible to examine a bibliographic description of a resource that is not a published monograph. This work is far from mature, but it reveals that OCLC's model of creative works encoded in Schema.org is potentially far richer than the evidence that can currently be discovered in legacy MARC records. The analysis is anchored in the data underlying the WorldCat.org record mentioned earlier describing a video of a live performance of Tchaikovsky's ballet *The Nutcracker* performed in 1987 at the Bolshoi Theater in Moscow. Similar examples are described in Smith-Yoshimura and Godby.[44]

The essential fields in the MARC source for this display are excerpted in figure 5.7. The 245 field contains title and creator of the performed work and the 260 field contains the name of the publisher of the DVD. The names of the primary stage performers are listed in the two 511 fields, from which a human reader can infer that the first 511 field has a list of dancers, while the second contains the name of the orchestra and conductor. Production credits for the performance, such as music, choreography, set design, and producer, are listed in the 508 field. The 650 fields indicate that the work is about ballet and mice. The 700 and 710 fields contain authority-controlled forms of some of the names listed in the 245, 508, and 511 fields.

Figure 5.8 is a graphical depiction of the most important RDF statements published on the WorldCat record. As in the previous example, the entity-relationship model expressed in RDF reveals the presence of two objects typed as "schema:CreativeWork"—a Manifestation-like description on the left and a Work-like description on the right, connected by the "schema:exampleOfWork"

245 04 $a The Nutcracker $h [videorecording]/ $c by Peter Tchaikovsky

260 __ $a [S.I.] : $b Arthaus Musiik, $c 1989

300 __ $a 1 videodisc (DVD) (101 nub,) : $b sd., col.,; $c 4 ¾ in.

511 1_ $a Natalya Arkhipova, Irek Mukhamedov, Yuri Vetrov, Bolshoi Ballet

511 0_ $a Bolshoi Theatre Orchestra conducted by Aleksandr Kopilov

508__ $a Producer, Takeshi Hara ; artistic director of the Bolshoi Ballet, Yuri Grigorovich ; director for NHK, Motoko Sakaguchi ; music by Pyotor Illyich Tchaikovsky ; scenario by Ivan Vsevolozhsky and Marius Petipa ; original choreography by Lev Ivanov ; revised choreography by Yuri Grigorovich.

650 $a Ballets.

700 $a Vetrov, Yuri

700 $a Arkhipova, Natalya.

700 $a Mukhamedov, Irek.

700 $a Kopilov, Aleksandr.

710 $a Videofilm/Bolshoi Theatre.

Figure 5.7 | **A MARC record for a video recording of *The Nutcracker*, WorldCat ID # 81750960**

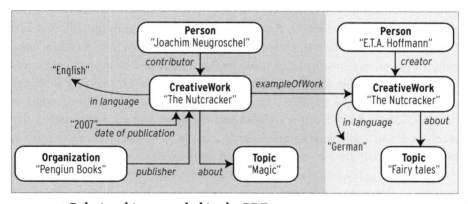

Figure 5.8 | **Relationships revealed in the RDF statements for the video recording of *The Nutcracker***

property. As in the first example, all of the RDF statements except literal strings such as titles and dates contain URIs in the subjects and predicates. But this RDF output is disappointing. The Manifestation description consists primarily of a long list of "schema:Person" and "schema:Organization" agents with a "schema:contributor" relationship to the creative work, while the Work description is a cluster of recorded performances of *The Nutcracker* at the Bolshoi Theater on multiple dates with an overlapping set of performers. The algorithm correctly associates E. T. A. Hoffmann with the ballet, but only accidentally because one of the records in the Work cluster mentions the relationship between the ballet and the E. T. A. Hoffmann fairy tale. The Manifestation description states that the language of the work is Russian, but real-world knowledge is required to infer that the performance of the ballet captured on the videodisc has some association, possibly erroneous, with a Russian-language libretto.

The model shown in figure 5.8 is best interpreted as a first-draft view of the entities and relationships that can be extracted from MARC records describing filmed performances. But the less-than-impressive result is a symptom of two unresolved problems.

First, the network of relationships is encoded primarily as free text in the 245, 260, 508, and 511 fields, not the controlled fields that are more recoverable algorithmically. Second, the conceptual model that underlies the MARC record works best for monographs and is not suited to the description of multimedia works with complex interdependencies among agents responsible for variations in content and execution. At OCLC, the free-text problem is being addressed in a research project that uses text-mining algorithms to extract roles from the free-text fields and match them with the names listed in the 700 and 710 fields, which would have the effect of upgrading the relationships from "contributor" to a more specific value using evidence supplied by human catalogers who contributed the source records to WorldCat. Though free text is always unpredictable, partial successes are possible because much of the content in the 245, 508, and 511 fields is stylized and can be parsed with a named-entity recognizer and a simple grammar. The data in the 511 field is easiest to process because it almost always contains a list of names delimited by commas. Once the names are extracted, the MARC semantics of the field enables a machine process to promote "contributors" to "performers." More subtly, a machine process can also infer the existence of an event in the underlying model because "schema:performer" is defined as a relationship between a "schema:Person" and a "schema:Event."[45]

Of course, a data-driven approach would be more effective if complemented with a top-down analysis that produces a richer model of the entities and relationships required for describing a filmed performance. An important start has been made in the study of audiovisual materials commissioned by the

Library of Congress.[46] After surveying the treatment of films by MARC, RDA, BIBFRAME, and more specialized standards used in audiovisual cataloging communities, the authors conclude that these materials are not adequately served by any current standard. An improved model would recognize that a film captures live action in elapsed time and can be interpreted as an event, though it is not always a product of the human imagination because it could be a singing bird or an unfolding natural disaster. Moreover, the production of a film requires agents acting in multiple roles, many of whom make primary contributions that are understated in data models such as MARC, FRBR, RDA, and BIBFRAME that draw a bright line between creators and contributors. Finally, the Library of Congress study recognizes that the physical artifacts of filmmaking exist in multiple versions and are often collected into aggregations.

Schema.org is also mentioned in the literature survey, but the report is sketchy on details about how audiovisual materials can be described with this standard. Nevertheless, OCLC's linked data researchers are confident that classes and properties defined in Schema.org, with minor extensions defined in BiblioGraph, can address many of the requirements specified in the Library of Congress study.

Figure 5.9 shows a high-level model for the filmed version of *The Nutcracker* inspired by the requirements specified in the study. Some of the features were first proposed by Mixter.[47] The model shows relationships among four creative works: the original Hoffmann fairy tale, the Tchaikovsky ballet, a performance of the ballet at the Bolshoi Theater, and a film of the performance recorded on a video object. All are assigned the type "schema:CreativeWork," subclasses such as "schema:Movie," or plausible BiblioGraph extensions such as "bgn:Ballet." As in the previous example, the creative work may have more than one type assignment that can be interpreted as an ontologically distinct facet. For example, the ballet performance is a creative work as well as a "schema:Event" because it is anchored in a time period during which a group of agents realize an artistic creation. Similarly, the video object is a creative work and a "schema:Product-Model" because it is a manufactured object with a model number that can be bought, sold, borrowed, and tracked. The creative works are linked through two properties defined in Schema.org, "schema:encodesCreativeWork" and "schema:workPerformed"—as well as the property "isBasedOn," which could be defined in BiblioGraph with a meaning equivalent to the corresponding RDA term that has been "unconstrained," or redefined to exclude a literal reference to the definitions of FRBR Work, Expression, Manifestation, and Item, as mentioned earlier.[48]

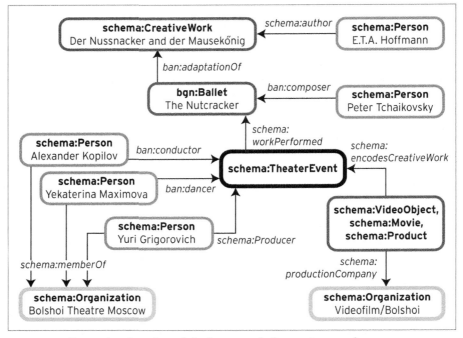

Figure 5.9 | **An aspirational model of a recorded creative work**

Once the four creative works have been identified, the agents can be distributed appropriately, clearing up a major source of confusion in the original MARC record and the RDF statements derived from it. Thus E. T. A. Hoffmann is the author of the fairy tale, Tchaikovsky is the composer of the ballet, Kopolov, Maximova, and Grigorovich are members of the Bolshoi Theater and performers in the theater event with identifiable roles, and Video-Film/Bolshoi is a distributor of the video object. Roles that are not defined in Schema.org, such as "composer," "conductor," or "dancer" could be defined in BiblioGraph. Or they could be entered as string values in a generic "Role" class, which as Wallis shows, permits a refinement or a narrower meaning for a defined role such as "contributor" or "performer."[49] Though the technical result is the same, the BiblioGraph representation would serve as a tool for negotiating with Schema.org to adopt a controlled list to which URIs might be assigned, thus anticipating that users on the broader Web might also need normalized terms to describe dancers, composers, and others involved in the production of a multimedia work.

The model shown in figure 5.9 is still a sketch because details that would be important to some users have been suppressed. But what is clear is that this example is dramatically more complex than the description of the memoir discussed earlier in this chapter, whose referent was a single creative work and whose properties could be specified through a set of lexical mappings directly from the MARC source. Though the model shown in figure 5.9 is not discoverable with current algorithms, it can at least be defined with relative ease in Schema.org and BiblioGraph by starting with the model developed for published monographs and enhancing it with a more complex network of relationships that results when identifiable acts of creation are realized as variant genres, content types, and physical realizations. As in the earlier examples, the core of the model is a set of creative works connected through relationships to one another and to the people and organizations that brought them into being.

The model also addresses two problems identified in the survey of options in the Library of Congress audiovisual study. The first is the assignment of "Agent" role relationships to the respective creative works. Without the constraints of a data model derived from FRBR, the model derived from Schema.org can simply name the "producer" relationship between Yuri Grigorovich and the performance, as well as all other Agent-Work relationships shown in figure 5.9, without having to consider whether the performance is a Work, Expression, or Manifestation, and whether Grigorovich is a primary creator or relegated to a contributor. This problem results only if properties are partitioned among Works, Expressions, Manifestations, and Items. But as the discussion of the RDF statements in figure 5.5 shows, most properties defined in OCLC's Semantic Web models of bibliographic description can float freely among these concepts. The result is the ontologically more natural set of statements asserting that a dancer is a primary creator of a performance event, a composer is the primary creator of a musical score, and an author is the primary creator of a fairy tale.

At a more abstract level, the authors of the audiovisual study argue that filmed works imply the existence of an event that unfolds in elapsed time, which is problematic for MARC and nearly every subsequently defined model of resource description that does not define "Event" as a primary concept. In Schema.org, "Event" is defined as a subclass of "schema:Thing," which implies an existence in multiple contexts that may or may not have a relationship with a creative work. The event implied in the *Nutcracker* description obviously does, but the same model could just as easily describe a video object that records a tsunami or a hurricane. The video object would still be a creative work with a producer and other human agents, but the event itself would not be doubly typed as "schema:CreativeWork" and would not be associated with identifiable human agents or have a traceable connection to another creative work. The network of relationships would be much simpler than that shown in figure 5.9.

CONCLUSION AND NEXT STEPS

The model for multimedia resources presented above is only a thumbnail sketch that shows the feasibility of expanding the use of Schema.org to describe a set of resources that are especially challenging and underserved by current library standards. It must be expanded to cover a broader range of examples and refined with input from the audiovisual cataloging community. Not coincidentally, these resources also show that OCLC's current strategy of populating linked data models through retrospective conversion are reaching an upper limit and will have to be upgraded—first, with more sophisticated text-mining algorithms and improved procedures for distinguishing high-quality data from errors, and ultimately with user interfaces that accompany the transformation of the data architecture for library metadata and support the yet-to-be-defined workflows of next-generation cataloging.

But the audiovisual model and the other examples discussed in this chapter also prescribe priorities for future development. In the modeling division of labor, we are still awaiting the specialist's view, which will define the vocabulary of curation for resources managed in cultural heritage institutions by experts with graduate degrees. As a result, current standards efforts in the library community are focused on the development of Semantic Web models of the ordinary-user view. Thus it is reasonable to point out that a cluster of creative works involving a fairy tale, a performance event, a ballet, a movie, and multiple agents can be described in Schema.org with a relatively small set of extensions. Given the intense public interest in recordings of multimedia performances, popular and authoritative resources such as the Internet Movie Database and MusicBrainz can be consulted to obtain additional clues for defining a model of such resources that is widely understood and may even turn out to be richer than current MARC models of audiovisual materials.[50] The resulting descriptions promise to facilitate discovery on the open Web because they would be expressed in the language that search engines can consume and would describe concepts that are important to the information-seeking public. And once all of the pieces are in place, the outcome will be a compelling demonstration of the benefits that accrue when libraries are more closely integrated into the Web, a goal to which the linked data paradigm is well-suited, and to which all of the library community's next-generation modeling effort aspires.

ACKNOWLEDGMENTS

This chapter describes work being done by a team of linked data experts at OCLC—in particular, Jon Fausey, Tod Matola, Jeff Mixter, Karen Smith-Yoshimura, Stephan Schindehette, Bruce Washburn, Richard Wallis, and Jeff Young. I have contributed to this effort. But I am solely responsible for the errors of analysis and perspective presented here.

Notes

1. Cathy de Rosa, Joanne Cantrell, Matthew Carlson, Peggy Gallagher, Janet Hawk, and Charlotte Sturtz, *Perceptions of Libraries: Context and Community,* a report to the OCLC membership (Dublin, OH: OCLC, 2010). www.oclc.org/content/dam/oclc/reports/2010perceptions/2010perceptions_all.pdf.

2. Library of Congress, *On the Record: Report of the Library of Congress Working Group on the Future of Bibliographic Control Library of Congress,* January 9, 2008, www.loc.gov/bibliographic-future/news/lcwg-ontherecord-jan08-final.pdf.

3. Schema, "Thing–>CreativeWork," 2015, http://schema.org/CreativeWork.

4. Carol Jean Godby, Shenghui Wang, and Jeffrey K. Mixter, *Library Linked Data in the Cloud: OCLC's Experiments with New Models of Library Resource Description: Synthesis Lectures in Linked Data and the Semantic Web,* 2015. A publication in the Morgan & Claypool Publishers series Synthesis Lectures on the Semantic Web: Theory and Technology. doi: 10.2200/S00620ED1V01Y201412WBE012.

5. Eric Miller and Bob Schloss, eds., "Resource Description Framework (RDF) Model and Syntax," Version 1, October 2, 1997, World Wide Web Consortium, www.w3.org/TR/WD-rdf-syntax-971002/; VIAF, "VIAF: Virtual International Authority File," 2014, http://viaf.org; FAST (Faceted Application of Subject Terminology), 2014, "FAST Linked Data: FAST Authority File," OCLC Experimental, http://experimental.worldcat.org/fast/; DDC. "Dewey Decimal Classification / Linked Data." 2014. OCLC. http://dewey.info.

6. Tim Berners-Lee, "Linked Data," in *Design Issues: Architectural and Philosophical Points,* July 27, 2006, World Wide Web Consortium, www.w3.org/DesignIssues/LinkedData.html.

7. Alistair Miles and Sean Bechhofer, "SKOS Simple Knowledge Organization System: Reference," W3C Recommendation, August 18, 2009, World Wide Web Consortium, www.w3.org/TR/2009/RECskos-reference-20090818/.

8. Ed Summers, Antoine Isaac, Clay Redding, and Dan Krech. "LCSH, SKOS, and Linked Data," in *DC-2008: Proceedings of the International Conference on Dublin Core and Metadata Applications*, 25–33, Berlin, Ger.: Dublin Core Metadata Initiative, 2008, http://edoc.huberlin.de/conferences/dc-2008/summers-ed-25/PDF/summers.pdf.

9. Thomas Baker, Emmanuelle Bermès, Karen Coyle, Gordon Dunsire, Antoine Isaac, Peter Murray, Michael Panzer, et al., "Library Linked Data Incubator Final Report," W3C Incubator Group Report, October 25, 2011, World Wide Web Consortium, www.w3.org/2005/Incubator/lld/XGR-lld-20111025/.

10. Tim Hodson, Corine Deliot, Alan Danskin, Heather Rosie, and Jan Ashton, "British Library Data Model – Book, V.1," British Library, August 4, 2012, www.bl.uk/bibliographic/pdfs/bldatamodelbook.pdf; Leigh Dodds, "An Introduction to the British National Bibliography, Part I," in *Lost Boy* (blog), October 28, 2014, http://blog.ldodds.com/2014/10/08/an-introduction-to-the-british-national-bibliography/.

11. BIBO, "The Bibliographic Ontology: Bibliographic Ontology Specification," 2009, http://bibliontology.com.

12. Gerard de Melo, "Lexvo.org Main Page," 2014, Lexvo.org. www.lexvo.org.

13. British Library, "Collection Metadata: Data Services," 2014, West Yorkshire, United Kingdom: British Library.

14. Google, "Introducing Schema.org: Search Engines Come Together for a Richer Web," in *Webmaster Central Blog: Official News on Crawling and Indexing Sites for the Google Index*, June 2, 2011, http://googlewebmastercentral.blogspot.com/2011/06/introducing-schemaorg-search-engines.html.

15. Dan Brickley, R.V. Guha, and Andrew Layman, "Resource Description Framework (RDF Schemas)," W3C working draft, April 9, 1998, World Wide Web Consortium, www.w3.org/TR/1998/WD-rdf-schema-19980409/.

16. Alan Morrison, Gabriel Kniesley, Marie Wallace, and Matt Everson, "Is Schema.org Good or Bad for the Semantic Web?" in Quora (online reference service), June 14–July 2, 2011, www.quora.com/Is-Schema-org-good-or-bad-for-the-Semantic-Web.

17. R. V. Guha, "What a Long, Strange Trip It's Been," presentation at the 2014 Semantic Technology and Business (SemTech) Conference, San Jose, CA, August 20, 2014, +www.slideshare.net/rvguha/sem-tech2014c.

18. Ian Hickson, "HTML Microdata," W3C working group note, October 29, 2013, World Wide Web Consortium, www.w3.org/TR/microdata/; Google, "Promote Your Content with Structured Data Markup," in *Google Developers*, February 12, 2015, https://developers.google.com/structured-data/?hl=ta&rd=1; Google, "Introducing the

Knowledge Graph: Things, Not Strings," in *Google Official Blog*, May 16, 2012, http://googleblog.blogspot.com/2012/05/introducing- knowledgegraph-things-not.html.

19. Martin Hepp, "GoodRelations: The Web Vocabulary for E-Commerce," 2014, www.heppnetz.de/projects/goodrelations/.

20. SBX, "Holdings via Offer," Schema Bib Extend Community Group, W3C Community and Business Groups, World Wide Web Consortium, 2014, www.w3.org/community/schemabibex/wiki/Holdings_via_Offer.

21. OCLC, "OCLC Adds Linked Data to WorldCat.org," OCLC news release, June 20, 2012, www.oclc.org/news/releases/2012/201238.en.html.

22. OCLC, "OCLC Research Activities and IFLA's Functional Requirements for Bibliographic Records," 2015, OCLC Research, www.oclc.org/research/activities/frbr .html; Barbara Tillett, "What Is FRBR? A Conceptual Model for the Bibliographic Universe," Library of Congress Cataloging Distribution Service, 2004, www.loc.gov/cds/downloads/FRBR.PDF.

23. W3C, "Semantic Web Development Tools," World Wide Web Consortium, 2014, www.w3.org/2001/sw/wiki/Tools.

24. SBX, "Schema Bib Extend Community Group," W3C Community and Business Groups, 2014, World Wide Web Consortium, www.w3.org/community/schemabibex/.

25. W3C, "public-schemabibex@w3.org: Mail Archives," last modified August 11, 2015, World Wide Web Consortium, https://lists.w3.org/Archives/Public/public -schemabibex/; W3C, "public-vocabs@w3.org: Mail Archives," last modified August 11, 2015, World Wide Web Consortium, https://lists.w3.org/Archives/Public/public -vocabs/2015Aug/author.html.

26. Dan Brickley and Libby Miller, "FOAF Vocabulary Specification 0.99," Namespace Document–Paddington Edition, January 14, 2014, http://xmlns.com/foaf/spec/.

27. Carol Jean Godby, "The Relationship between BIBFRAME and OCLC's Linked-Data Model of Bibliographic Description: A Working Paper," 2013, http://oclc.org/content/dam/research/publications/library/2013/2013–05.pdf.

28. Schema, "Extension Mechanism," 2015, https://schema.org/docs/extension.html.

29. Hilary Putnam, "Meaning and Reference," in *Naming, Necessity, and Natural Kinds*, ed. Stephan P. Schwartz (Ithaca, NY: Cornell University Press, 1977), 119–34.

30. Leo Sauermann and Richard Cyganiac, "Cool URIs for the Semantic Web," W3C Interest Group note, December 3, 2005, World Wide Web Consortium, www.w3.org/TR/cooluris/.

31. Library of Congress, "BIBFRAME AV Modeling Study: Defining a Flexible Model for Description of Audiovisual Resources," last modified May 15, 2014, www.loc.gov/bibframe/pdf/bibframe-avmodelingstudy-may15–2014.pdf.

32. Godby, Wang, and Mixter, *Library Linked Data in the Cloud*. doi: 10.2200/S00620ED 1V01Y201412WBE012.

33. RDA (Resource Description and Access), "RDA Toolkit: Resource Description and Access," 2010, www.rdatoolkit.org.

34. RDA, "RDA Element Sets: Unconstrained Properties," RDA Registry, last modified April 7, 2015, www.rdaregistry.info/Elements/u/.

35. Library of Congress, "240—Uniform Title (NR)," in *MARC 21 Format for Bibliographic Data, 1999 Edition*, Network Development and MARC Standards Office, Library of Congress, 2014, www.loc.gov/marc/bibliographic/bd130.html.

36. Karen Smith-Yoshimura, "Multilingual Bibliographic Structure," OCLC research update at the Annual Conference of the American Library Association, Las Vegas, NV, June 30, 2014, OCLC Research, YouTube video, https://www.youtube.com/watch?v=NG1tkE03WJo.

37. Karen Smith-Yoshimura and Carol Jean Godby, "An OCLC Perspective on What It Takes to Make Linked Data Work," presentation at the ALCTS ALA Preconference, "Beyond the Looking Glass: Real World Data: What Does It Take to Make It Work?" San Francisco, CA, June 26, 2015.

38. Library of Congress, "Code List for Relators," Network Development and MARC Standards Office, last modified May 13, 2010, www.loc.gov/marc/relators/.

39. Tillett, "What Is FRBR?" www.loc.gov/cds/downloads/FRBR.PDF.

40. OCLC, "OCLC Releases WorldCat Works as Linked Data," OCLC news release, April 28, 2014, https://www.oclc.org/news/releases/2014/201414dublin.en.html.

41. Godby, Wang, and Mixter, *Library Linked Data in the Cloud*. doi: 10.2200/S00620 ED1V01Y201412WBE012.

42. Tillett, "What Is FRBR?" www.loc.gov/cds/downloads/FRBR.PDF.

43. RDA, "RDA Toolkit: Resource Description and Access," 2010, www.rdatoolkit.org.

44. Smith-Yoshimura and Godby, "An OCLC Perspective on What It Takes to Make Linked Data Work."

45. Schema, "Thing–>Property>Performer," 2015, http://schema.org/performer.

46. Library of Congress, "BIBFRAME AV Modeling Study: Defining a Flexible Model for Description of Audiovisual Resources," last modified May 15, 2014, www.loc.gov/bibframe/pdf/bibframe-avmodelingstudy-may15–2014.pdf.

47. Jeffrey K. Mixter, "Linked Data in VRA Core 4.0: Converting VRA XML Records into RDF/XML," thesis submitted to the College of Communication and Information in partial fulfillment of the M.S. and M.L.I.S. degrees, Kent State University, 2013, http://jmixter.s3-website-us-east-1.amazonaws.com/thesis/LinkedDataInVRACore4.pdf.

48. RDA (Resource Description and Access), "RDA Element Sets: Unconstrained Properties," RDA Registry, last modified April 7, 2015, www.rdaregistry.info/Elements/u/.

49. Richard Wallis, "The Role of Role in Schema.org," in *Data Liberate* (blog), April 15, 2014, http://dataliberate.com/2014/09/a-step-for-schema-orga-leap-for-bib-data-on-the-web/.

50. IMDB, "IMDb" (Internet Movie Database), 2015, www.imdb.com; MB, "MusicBrainz," 2015, https://musicbrainz.org/.

6

BIBFRAME AND LINKED DATA FOR LIBRARIES

Sally H. McCallum

oday "linked data" has become a key goal of our Internet-based environment and libraries are active with investigation, experimentation, and trial and error. However, just what is meant by "linked data" and how it will transform the user experience are not entirely clear. A basic definition is "relating data in one base to data in another." This is not a new concept to librarians since they have been doing linking for years without the tools or concepts of today, by linking with strings (such as names or subjects) or codes (such as language codes) or numbers (such as ISBNs). Now the World Wide Web Consortium (W3C) that makes the rules and advances the Web and Internet environment has developed models, principles, tools, and components that enable linking to be more dynamic by using universal resource identifiers (URIs) that can be automatically followed to reveal much more about an entity—and where further links may be found or inferences made to gather more information. This reflects the linked data principles articulated by Tim Berners-Lee in 2006: use URIs to name things; make them HTTP URIs so machines can look them up; when looked up, provide useful information using linked data standards such as the resource description framework (RDF) and the search language, SPARQL; include links to other URIs.[1] So linking is not new to bibliographic data but linked data via URIs is, and it holds interesting potential for libraries.

In 2007, at about the same time that Berners-Lee was explaining linked data, the Library of Congress (LC) organized a community inquiry into the "future of bibliographic control" that became a catalyst for exploration and change. A wide-ranging report, *On the Record: Report of the Library of Congress Working Group on the Future of Bibliographic Control,* was written by a committee and some major recommendations were made. Some have been acted upon, such as the testing and subsequent implementation of the cataloging rules Resource Description and Access (RDA).[2] Others are still on the table such as a rethinking of subject vocabularies. But two technical recommendations were ideally suited for exploration using the emerging linked data framework of the W3C. They are the following.

USE TECHNOLOGY TO GET BROADER USE OF LIBRARY-CURATED VOCABULARIES

Begin transitioning LC-managed vocabularies to a platform that is both web services-friendly and allows files to be downloaded for incorporation into other applications. These vocabularies include the many lists that are used in bibliographic records such as language and geographic codes, resource format codes, and so on. Contribute resources to support the work of coordinating the definitions and linkages of data elements in nationally and internationally accepted bibliographic standards. Generate standard web-based identifiers for all data elements and vocabularies that LC maintains.[3]

REPLACE THE MARC FORMAT WITH A DATA INTERCHANGE FRAMEWORK THAT MAKES LIBRARY DATA MORE READILY AVAILABLE ON THE WEB

Recognizing that Z39.2/MARC are no longer fit for the purpose, work with the library and other interested communities to specify and implement a carrier for bibliographic information that is capable of representing the full range of data of interest to libraries, and of facilitating the exchange of such data both within the library community and with related communities. Data that are stored in separate library databases often do not disclose themselves to web applications, and thus do not appear in searches carried out through commonly used search engines. New and anticipated uses of bibliographic data require a format that will accommodate and distinguish expert-, automated-, and user-generated metadata, including annotations (reviews, comments) and usage data. Flexible design should allow for the selective (modular) use of metadata in different environments.[4]

Linked data concepts were not mentioned in the *Future of Bibliographic Control* report because the terminology was just being coined, although the concepts had been discussed in the W3C in the context of the Semantic Web since the late 1990s.

In 2007 the Library of Congress was already starting on the first of these tasks, thus the recommendations of the report were timely. The LC was investigating the linked data framework for standards and models for exposing its vocabularies such as the Library of Congress Subject Headings (LCSH). Accordingly, the LCSH was made publicly available as linked data in 2009 followed by name authorities, countries, languages, and many other controlled lists used in bibliographic standards such as MARC, MODS, and PREMIS. This project, Library of Congress Linked Data Service, is commonly called ID.[5] Its aim is to establish stable identifiers in URI form for entities and concepts that are useful for description of cultural heritage material. The URIs lead to data expressed in a way that enables its consumption in the linked data environment, that is, in RDF.

Then in 2011, Deanna Marcum, then the associate librarian for library services at the Library of Congress, announced the start of the Bibliographic Framework Initiative (subsequently labeled BIBFRAME) to respond to the second major technical recommendation of the *Future of Bibliographic Control* report: to replace MARC for interchange and to make library resources more visible on the Web.[6]

The Library of Congress, with the library community, is tackling the challenges described above. This chapter looks at five aspects of that development:

- Using RDF
- Library of Congress Linked Data Service
- Developing BIBFRAME
- Models
- Experiencing

USING RDF

Since RDF is a key building block of this whole development, an introduction to the special characteristics that make it useful will illustrate its differences from today's common data interchange standards such as MARC.

RDF TRIPLES AND SERIALIZATIONS

At its simplest, RDF is about triples, which can be thought of in terms of a basic grammatical sentence; it has three parts: subject, verb, and object. For example, the sentence: "Bambi is a deer" has three parts: subject "Bambi," verb "is a," object "deer." A triple in RDF is usually referred to as a "statement."

The "RD" in "RDF" is "Resource Description." Essentially, one starts with a *resource,* and describes it with statements. A resource is anything identified by a URI, thus:

- Virtually anything can have a URI, so virtually anything can be a resource.
- The resource description will be a set of triples (i.e., sentences or statements).

The verb part of an RDF triple is usually not referred to as a verb, but rather a "property," "predicate," or "relationship." These three things have different meanings; "property" and "relationship" are used for different types of objects, and "predicate" is a generalization of those two.

In order for the triples to be consumable by a computer, the triples have to be represented in a commonly understood format that a computer can recognize and process. This is a familiar concept as MARC has at least two such format structures, ISO 2709 and XML. For RDF there are a number of these formats in use, called "RDF serializations." Consider the novel *Cannery Row.* It is a resource, in fact it is a BIBFRAME resource, and specifically, a BIB-FRAME Work. As such, it has a URI: http://bibframe.example.org/44040225. In constructing triples describing this resource, this URI is used as the subject for these triples. Example statements (in plain English, not RDF syntax) are provided below:

http://bibframe.example.org/44040225 is a BIBFRAME Work.

http://bibframe.example.org/44040225 is a BIBFRAME Text.

http://bibframe.example.org/44040225 has title "Cannery row".

http://bibframe.example.org/44040225 has creator "Steinbeck, John, 1902-1968".

http://bibframe.example.org/44040225 has subject "Marine biologists—Fiction".

http://bibframe.example.org/44040225 has subject "Community life—Fiction".

http://bibframe.example.org/44040225 has classification "PZ3.S8195".

Applying a serialization to this set of RDF triples that describe the resource *Cannery Row,* we get the following.

The first two statements specify types for this resource. Any resource may have more than one type, and in this case it is a BIBFRAME Work and it is also a BIBFRAME Text (as opposed, for example, to a Moving Image). These types are called "classes" in RDF, and BIBFRAME Text is a subclass of BIBFRAME Work (which means that any BIBFRAME Text is a BIBFRAME Work). The terms Work and Text, class names in the BIBFRAME ontology, are referred to as bf:Work and bf:Text to denote that they are being used within the context of the BIBFRAME ontology, and not some other ontology that might also use these terms but with a different meaning. Also the verb expression "is a" is abbreviated as just "a"; this is well-known within all of RDF to denote "is of type." Finally, URIs within RDF triples are enclosed with angle brackets. So the first two statements from above are rewritten as follows:

    <http://bibframe.example.org/44040225>   a bf:Work.
    <http://bibframe.example.org/44040225>   a bf:Text.

The remaining statements, "has title," "has creator," "has subject," and "has classification" are simplified in BIBFRAME to bf:title, bf:creator, bf:subject, and bf:classification. In the example above, the objects in these are literals and not classes or URIs, and the convention is to place literal strings in quotation marks. Also note that the RDF conventions that class names begin with upper case and predicates begin with lowercase are followed in the BIBFRAME ontology.

There are also writing conventions that the subject does not need to be repeated when two triples have the same subject; and when consecutive triples not only have the same subject, but also have the same predicate, the predicate does not need to be repeated. Semicolons (";") separate the first and commas

(",") the second condition. The whole statement for a subject ends with a period
("."). So the description, consisting of seven triples, is rewritten as follows:

> \<http://bibframe.example.org/44040225> a bf:Work , bf:Text ; bf:title "Cannery row" ;
>   bf:creator "Steinbeck, John, 1902–1968" ;
>
> bf:subject "Marine biologists—Fiction" , "Community life—Fiction" ;
>
> bf:classification "PZ3.S8195."

Although the description has been reduced to five lines, there are still
eight triples. This serialization is called Terse RDF Triple Language, or Turtle.

LITERALS, URIS, AND RDF

The triples that make up the description of *Cannery Row* and their serialization
shown above illustrate two types of objects in RDF statements, literals, and
URIs. When the object is a URI the information itself is not the object but
it points with the URI to another RDF resource that does contain the information. For example, instead of the literal "Steinbeck, John, 1902–1968," the
object of that triple might have been a URI that pointed to an RDF description of John Steinbeck and that included more information about him than
his name and birth and death date. An alternative to pointing to the sought
information is to bring it into the description, and this is often referred to as
having a "blank node" as the object of the triple.

Since many of the characteristics of RDF are commonplace and could be
illustrated by the MARC format, what are the advantages to moving to this
new method of expressing descriptions? First of all, this is a structure that is
being embraced for data across communities. The Web itself set the precedent
for this as HTML and its successors were adopted by all to provide information on the Web.

Currently, the conventional way to link to, for example, a richer description of John Steinbeck, which librarians do include in some of their MARC
authority records, is by the "authorized" data string for his name or by identifiers.
While these linking keys are not usually machine-actionable except within
an internal system, the URI system that was built for the Internet is a vehicle
that enables a machine to find the richer information no matter where it is.

And finally, the conventions for describing the ontology properties and
classes that are used for RDF statements are also machine-understandable

to a large extent. Thus the amount of "thought" that a machine can bring to information is greatly enhanced. In some situations a machine can start to make relations and connections that are not explicit in the data, called inferencing.

So using RDF and following W3C and Internet standards opens up greater possibilities for the use of library-produced data. This new and complex form of linking data is in its early stages and libraries are getting in to the new environment early. Library use of these conventions can be explored and can grow as the Internet develops linked data guidelines.

LIBRARY OF CONGRESS LINKED DATA SERVICE (ID)

With the above introduction to the cornerstone standard for the linked data environment, RDF, let's explore how it is used in the BIBFRAME project. The first step was to make the many large (LCSH, Name Authority File, etc.) and small (language codes, content and media terms, etc.) controlled lists available for use in a linked data application. These many controlled vocabularies and lists used for bibliographic description needed to be transformed from their printed or web forms into RDF so their links can be referenced by URIs and their descriptions can be made accessible in RDF. Making those links both automatic and enhanced is the aim of the Library of Congress Linked Data Service, which began development in 2008 with LCSH and continues in the BIBFRAME project, adding bibliographic vocabularies and lists that are needed to make RDF bibliographic descriptions for library material.[7]

To transform this data to RDF a vocabulary or "ontology" with appropriate properties and classes was needed. This is a familiar concept to librarians because in the MARC environment MARC itself is a vocabulary, although expressed in a totally different way, with tags and indicators and subfield codes being roughly analogous to properties and classes.

In the Library of Congress's linked data projects two ontologies have been evolving to support traditional bibliographic data: BIBFRAME, with properties and classes related to bibliographic description data; and MADS for classes and properties related to authority and list data. The ontology closely related to the ID service is MADSRDF (Metadata Authority Description Schema in RDF).[8] It provides a data model that is suitable for the types of authority, code, and term lists used in bibliographic data.

The BIBFRAME project uses the ontologies that are especially suited to library data, such as special structures found in name and subject files, but it also uses elements from other ontologies where that is appropriate. The W3C developed several foundation ontologies for RDF: OWL (Web Ontology Language), RDF, and RDFS (RDF Schema). They contain basic properties that are important in building any OWL-based RDF ontology. The W3C has also produced a basic thesaurus ontology, SKOS (Simple Knowledge Organization System), which has become widely used, and several others that may be important in the future.[9] The BIBFRAME and MADSRDF vocabularies draw on these and other well-established and presumably stable ontologies.

MADSRDF, the principal ontology used in ID, is closely related to SKOS. The more complex data structures used in bibliographic data are not supported in SKOS, intentionally, because it is intended for broad application, but the MADSRDF ontology is fully mapped to SKOS in the RDF that supports the ontology. This enables interoperability of MADSRDF data with the broader, less detailed SKOS standard. For example, a madsrdf:Authority is a subclass of skos:Concept.

Another feature of MADSRDF is the separation of the information that provides *labeling* of the concept being described, and, in the case of names, information that more appropriately describes aspects of the "real world object" (RWO) that the label addresses. For example, in the case of a person, a property such as madsrdf:authoritativeLabel relates to the person's name, John Steinbeck, 1902–1968, while RWO information such as madsrdf:fieldOfActivity describes the person, a novelist.

After starting with the Library of Congress Subject Headings, ID has been expanded to include the cooperative name authority file and the primary code and term lists used in bibliographic data.

ID has also been expanded to support the value lists found in the PREMIS standard for preservation of bibliographic data. This enables experimentation in the community with linked data related to preservation because these lists are accessible and referencable in RDF for institutions to use in data format and storage configurations.

DEVELOPING BIBFRAME

Changing Environment

With the terminology component started, the next step toward a linked data environment was to restructure the bibliographic descriptions themselves, which are the heart of bibliographic control. There were many motivators for taking this step, one being MARC itself.[10] It was certainly the case that MARC had moved as best it could with the times. It had been adapted to different cataloging conventions—AACR (Anglo American Cataloguing Rules) and earlier rules, archival descriptions, different media needs, holdings complications, and conventions of other countries such as Canada, the United Kingdom, and Germany. It had even developed technically, moving from limited character sets to embrace UNICODE and enabling an XML structure in addition to the traditional ISO 2709 structure for bibliographic descriptions.[11] Not to mention that it fully permeated the bibliographic environment because it provided the core data for integrating acquisitions, cataloging, online public catalogs, and record sharing and resource lending systems.

But this extensive reach and long-term use also bred an amazing accumulation of data elements—and these ran up against some structural limitations in the tagging and subfield coding in the ISO 2709 structure. MARCXML provided structural expansion but not without loss when converting to the traditional structure.[12] It was also not easy to adapt to replacing data with links via URIs.

At the same time, cataloging practices have been changing, with the most disruptive change being the introduction of a new cataloging norm for libraries, RDA. RDA has an increased emphasis on relationships, a natural for linked data. Other developments include new consideration of how much "transcription" is needed versus standardizing the information for retrieval needs. Bibliographic control practices are also adding into records pointers to many "nontraditional" resources in records such as cover images, tables of contents, reviews, abstracts, author biographies, and content excerpts—the Amazon effect.

Other developments in the broader community have also provided impetus for format redevelopment. There have been several resource modeling projects in the last fifteen or so years with FRBR (Functional Requirements for Bibliographic Records), <indecs> metadata framework, and CIDOC Conceptual Reference Model, to name a few. FRBR was used as the model behind RDA.[13]

The nature of library collections has also been shifting to electronic resources and to more media resources like recorded sound and moving images, even as the printed resource production has not yet diminished. And finally, library systems have been challenged to provide more functionality: access management (licensing and rights) for electronic resources and object management to preserve both analog and electronic resources.

All of the above factors have both stressed the MARC format itself and argued for a new resource description and interchange environment.

BIBFRAME Goals

With these motivations the community was ready for the launch of an exploration of a new framework for bibliographic control, which was called for in the *Future of Bibliographic Control* report described earlier. The goals of the Bibliographic Framework Initiative (BIBFRAME) are ambitious. Just as MARC had tried to accommodate different cataloging norms and various media, the new initiative needs to be as open to different norms and models and media as possible.

Many types of bibliographic control data, not just description, needed to be reconsidered in a new environment. The key areas of description, authority, and holdings might be reconfigured, coded data appears to be a natural for conversion to links, and the relationship between pre-coordinated subject headings and subject terms could be studied. And all that data that had often been pushed into MARC as the only carrier solution needed to be rethought—technical metadata, preservation metadata, rights, and special archival data.

Also, the Internet environment might yield different configurations for data exchange, for internal storage, and for input interfaces and techniques. In the MARC environment the internal storage bore similarities to the format, so that the data could be output without loss. And the input interfaces also had the flavor of the MARC field and subfield tags and arrangements, so that those aspects of the MARC format became a sort of meta-language for catalogers. It is likely that exchange formats will be less obvious, at least at the interface level in the BIBFRAME environment.

A general requirement was that whereas traditional linking had been done with textual data strings and identifier, URIs had to be the linking goal of any new environment. Other goals included the accommodation of different types of libraries—large, small, research, public, and specialized. Since scholarship requires access to the knowledge generated in the past, so existing bibliographic descriptions—for example, over 330 million at OCLC—needed to be able to be brought forward to the new environment. It was also realized the change was so enormous and potentially costly that there would be a long transition, so MARC needed adequate maintenance and support until it might no longer be needed.

BIBFRAME Development

The Library of Congress tackled the project via various initiatives. The first was contractual support to develop a high-level model for a new environment,

"Bibliographic Framework as a Web of Data: Linked Data Model and Supporting Services."[14] Eric Miller, who had worked with OCLC and its Dublin Core initiative and with the W3C during its development of RDF, was the contractor, with his company Zepheira. As soon as his report was complete and published on the Web in late 2012, a small group of institutions were invited to work with filling it out and taking it to the next level. This expert group included representatives from OCLC, the National Library of Medicine, Princeton University, George Washington University, the British Library, and the Deutsche Bibliothek. For a year there was simultaneous consideration of the model by this group and by the community via an electronic discussion list, BIBFRAME.[15] The community was just beginning to take serious notice of linked data requirements for a new environment, so the year was one of more questions than answers.

In order to enable the community to have a glimpse of what the model meant, the Library of Congress developed a "starter" BIBFRAME ontology, taking advice from needs expressed in the MARC environment, from RDA which was just beginning to be implemented, and from RDF conventions that were current at the time. The LC then developed various tools based on that ontology to enable a concrete look at BIBFRAME data. Since there was initially no editing system to create new BIBFRAME descriptions, the focus had to be on converting existing MARC data to BIBFRAME descriptions. With the MARC-to-BIBFRAME transformation tool a MARC record can be transformed to a simple BIBFRAME description. A BIBFRAME editor interface for inputting BIBFRAME descriptions was also developed jointly with Zepheira. But those and other tools are simple and incomplete because elaborate development needed to wait until the experimentation pointed out where revisions and changes to approaches were needed. The tools have been put into GitHub, a public web-based online hosting environment used primarily for program code, for others to download and experiment with them.[16] The community has been very responsive to a request to submit comments and corrections in the GitHub reporting space.

MARC, BIBFRAME, AND RDA MODELS

The MARC model is a good starting point for understanding the fundamentals of the BIBFRAME model. It is familiar to most librarians working in the bibliographic control areas of libraries. The MARC model at a "high level" has three principal components: Bibliographic, Authority, and Holdings. The data in the bibliographic component is a description of the resource being cataloged—both its conceptual (FRBR/RDA work and expression) and its physical embodiment (FRBR/RDA manifestation).

Authority data holds the authorized forms of names of persons, corporate bodies, and conferences, and of subject headings made up of topics, temporals, and places. Its emphasis is on the *names* of those resources, as the name strings are used to both link resources and to present browse displays to users. But it also contains the authorized names for titles, called uniform titles, which relate to works and expressions in the FRBR/RDA context. These authorized forms of names, subjects, and titles are used in the bibliographic records as needed. And finally the MARC holdings component provides the information on how much an institution holds of the resource and where it is located, along with lending and acquisition information. Figure 6.1 illustrates this current configuration of description information under MARC with the FRBR/RDA model on the right.

As is illustrated, the FRBR/RDA work and expression components are split between the MARC Authority and Bibliographic layers. The BIBFRAME model moves the bibliographic data closer to the FRBR/RDA view of bibliographic resources, as is illustrated in figure 6.2.

The BIBFRAME Work class, bf:Work, which is the conceptual view of a resource, relates to the FRBR/RDA Work and Expression entities. The BIBFRAME Instance class is the physical embodiment of a Work which corresponds to FRBR/RDA manifestations. The BIBFRAME Authority class

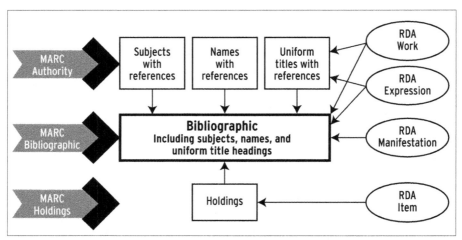

Figure 6.1 | **MARC data model with RDA mapping**

provides information for key concepts with defined relationships to Works and Instances. The Item class covers the typical information concerning items that are held. This class has been variously treated as an Annotation and as a part of the Instance during experimentation but appears to fit best as its own class. The Annotation class is a flexible add-on to Works, Instances, Authorities, and Items that can be used for comments and reviews of resources—and other information to be explored. Figure 6.2 illustrates the BIBFRAME model in relation to the FRBR/RDA high-level model.

There are striking differences from MARC in the BIBFRAME model, and the most prominent is modeling uniform title authority records as Work descriptions. The RDA model on the right of the diagram in figure 6.2 shows that RDA works and expressions are BIBFRAME Works, not title authorities. Treating them as Works is appropriate and it enables them to have subjects associated with them. The different manifestations of a Work are separately described as Instances and then linked to the Work information. Thus in a linked data environment the "authorized" uniform title name does not need to be recorded in the manifestation description—just the link to it. It also means that all manifestations (BIBFRAME Instances) *must* have a Work to relate to, and in the past uniform title authority records were only created when certain conditions applied. Moreover, in the MARC environment it was common to try to describe on one record the manifestation and all the different carriers for it. With the BIBFRAME model the expectation is that

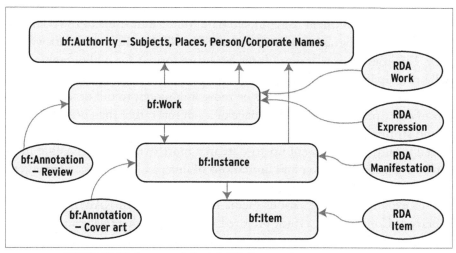

Figure 6.2 | **BIBFRAME data model with RDA mapping**

major differences in carriers, such as print and electronic, would be separate Instances of a Work and characteristics of each can then be clearly recorded in the Instance descriptions.

In BIBFRAME there is the intent to treat "authorities" as more than a place to record an authorized name string, as was noted in an earlier section. The authority descriptions include dual information—the "authorized" form of the name of the entity and a description of the entity, the "real world object." So in the case of a person entity, the traditional name and name-related cross-references would be available, but information about the person behind the name would also be available, such as the birth date, occupation, gender, and so on. While some of these attributes of the person may also be used in the preferred form of the name, that choice is up to the cataloger.

Thus a benefit of using the URI rather than the name string to identify and link entities is that information about the entity is available (in RDF) at the place where the URI points, in addition to the preferred form of the name. This follows the fundamental tenets of linked data that "things" should be identified by URIs that when de-referenced (i.e., followed) will provide information in RDF about the entity. It is also compatible with the RDA data model.

MANY QUESTIONS

BIBFRAME is modeled with a careful look at the various emerging models of the bibliographic community, fitting them into the current worldview of the Internet environment using linked data "rules." But some of the common practices for bibliographic data do not match well with the linked data worldview. This transition to a more Internet-aware format for bibliographic data will bring up issues for how the community carries on its business. One issue will be the use of links. Will there be more linking out to full descriptions or bits of descriptions (such as a language or a subject) rather than bringing them in and storing them locally? How will indexing and retrieval work? If data is stored locally, can it be kept up-to-date in a more dynamic way? What links can be trusted? The power and limitations of links will have to be worked out with experience and experimentation.

To explore the fit of various media to the basic BIBFRAME model the Library of Congress had a study prepared analyzing moving image and recorded sound material, two primary types of audiovisual resources. The study was entitled "BIBFRAME AV Modeling Study: Defining a Flexible Model for

Description of Audiovisual Resources."[17] The Library of Congress is particularly interested in these media as it has very large and varied collections of them due to the LC's large preservation commitment at its Packard Campus for Audio Visual Conservation in Culpeper, Virginia. The study pointed to a general fit with the model with an important exception—the treatment of events. Thus a further study of events and other points identified by the study will be needed. Reconciling those media, and other resources that are very different from "book-oriented" material, with a common model will be a challenge, but this could greatly improve access to those materials versus the current MARC environment.

Another issue or opportunity will be to use multiple authority files when creating descriptions. This could have the potential to reduce the cost of maintaining authority files and, as a "bonus," specialized community authority files might contain more information than libraries can afford to gather. Currently BIBFRAME enables the specification of multiple authority pointers for an entity, but how many and which ones may not be easy to determine.

As part of its focus on relationships, RDA put more emphasis on specifying the role a person or corporate body played in the creation of a resource. While the cataloging community has had an extensive role list for many years associated with MARC, it was only sporadically employed in cataloging operations. Now with new prominence for roles, the RDA list of roles has been reconciled with the larger MARC list and the new environment could make it easier to apply role information more consistently. However, questions remain. There are other specialized role lists, for example, for moving image, music, and other specialized communities. Do guidelines need to be determined to establish consistency; are hierarchies needed; and what are the retrieval aspects of roles from different lists? The specification of roles when creating bibliographic descriptions has the potential to enhance end-user retrieval and understanding of those descriptions.

Another type of relationship that is also more prominent in RDA and in linked data is between resources such as Work to Work and Instance to Instance. They have been recorded at a high level in MARC (e.g., other edition), with the serial relationships in MARC being the most explicit (e.g., absorbed in part). There is an extensive list in RDA, some with great detail (e.g., musical variations based on). And of course the new environment needs to be able to accommodate new lists from other communities. How much reconciliation of different lists will be needed? How do we want to treat these relationships for retrieval and for display?

There are myriad smaller issues that linked data brings to the surface for consideration. Should we split Instances by carrier or just by different media: different BIBFRAME Instances for the paperback, hardback, library binding, print, electronic, and audio books or just for print, electronic, and audio? Can we develop authority descriptions for more entities, such as publisher names? One can imagine an environment where publishers maintain such lists of their imprints and make them available as linked data with information about and a standard name for the imprint.

These and other issues should be explored in the coming years as libraries try out and analyze their data from the linked data point of view. Some changes will be needed in the way and what data is recorded, and adjustments to the traditional systems will need to be worked out.

EXPERIENCING

Time to Find Out

One way this new approach to exchange of our bibliographic data can be tested and explored is to actually implement on a pilot scale. At the time this chapter was written, a pilot was under way at the Library of Congress to test some aspects of BIBFRAME. It began in the third quarter of 2015. Pilot participants—Library of Congress catalogers—are inputting BIBFRAME data, comparing it to MARC, and exploring links. The scope of the pilot is ambitious, with the following preparations undertaken.

The BIBFRAME file for the pilot is the Library of Congress bibliographic and authority records converted to BIBFRAME descriptions. The MARC bibliographic records were split by machine into Work and Instance descriptions. This first required that the title and name/title uniform title records in the MARC authority file be converted to BIBFRAME Work descriptions. Then the MARC bibliographic file was transformed to create Instance descriptions. The MARC bibliographic records *with uniform titles* were linked to the BIB-FRAME Work descriptions created from the MARC title authority records and the subjects and other Work information in the bibliographic records was moved to the Work descriptions. The remainder of the MARC bibliographic record became Instance descriptions. Those MARC Bibliographic records that *did not have uniform titles* were split apart into Work descriptions (title, subjects, classification, etc.) and Instance descriptions (the rest). There was also an attempt made to break apart the new Instances that have print and electronic mixed and make separate Instances. This was difficult due to past (and current) practices, but determining the feasibility is one of the pilot goals. This created an imperfect but usable file of linked BIBFRAME Work and Instance descriptions.

Another major component of the pilot is the editor that is used by the catalogers to create new descriptions directly as BIBFRAME descriptions. Here the programmers started with the simple editor that was made available on GitHub. The programmers added to it a profile editor, which enabled creation of profiles (or templates) for catalogers to use to adapt the data elements suggested by the system to ones needed for the material at hand. Also, a search component was added for the editor that enables catalogers to search the converted BIBFRAME file. They can then create new Instances if BIBFRAME Works are found, or create both BIBFRAME Works and BIBFRAME Instances if not. There are many features of a basic input module that are still to be experimented with, such as pulling descriptions from external systems and linking to external systems for information. However, the pilot editor provides look up and type ahead during input.

In the pilot the cataloger is not working with input screens that use numbers and codes for data elements as does the typical MARC-based system input screen, but uses labels for the elements. This is one way the future environment will be very different from the current one, as the cataloger may not need to know as much about the "format" that holds the data than with MARC. This new form of input screen is an area that will create interesting experimentation. Also, increasingly, there will be data components of descriptions that can become URIs that point to more information than just the "string." The challenge will be to sort out what is useful and what is not.

The third major area that the LC is working on for the pilot is enhancement of the Library of Congress Linked Data Service (ID) (described earlier) to contain more of the standardized data needed in descriptions, so that elements will have URIs and RDF descriptions. As was noted, the person, corporate, and subject files are already maintained in ID as RDF as are some basic lists such as languages, countries, and organizations. As planning went forward more lists were added to enable the BIBFRAME descriptions to be as rich with links as possible to help in evaluating this aspect of linked bibliographic data.

GOING FORWARD

The *Future of Bibliographic Control* report that recommended serious reconsideration of the library data interchange environment came just as the W3C was giving new life to its earlier Semantic Web concepts. The present chapter has described briefly a major component of that new environment, RDF, and the attempt through the Bibliographic Framework Initiative of the Library of Congress to test how linked data could enhance the library experience. The amount of change will be enormous but the Library of Congress is trying by sharing tools, ontology work, and experiences to facilitate community exploration. In just a few years librarians have become much more knowledgeable about the precepts of a linked data scenario, placing them in a position to delve into this change. Another major step is for the vendors that supply many of the services in the community to start to explore linked data, because they are the community's essential innovators, and that has begun. In the 1960s and 1970s the AACR cataloging rules and MARC format for bibliographic data were developed. Forty years later we are in the transition to new cataloging rules and also a new carrier environment with RDA and BIBFRAME.

ACKNOWLEDGMENTS

The description of RDF in the "Using RDF" section of this chapter is adapted from material prepared by Ray Denenberg for the BIBFRAME plot project.

Notes

1. Tim Berners-Lee, "Linked Data," 2006, www.w3.org/DesignIssues/LinkedData.html.
2. *On the Record: Report of the Library of Congress Working Group on the Future of Bibliographic Control*, January 9, 2008, Washington, DC: Library of Congress, 2008, www.loc.gov/bibliographic-future/news/lcwg-ontherecord-jan08-final.pdf; *RDA: Resource Description & Access* (Chicago: American Library Association, 2010). Official content resides in the RDA Toolkit.
3. *Future of Bibliographic Control*, 15.
4. Ibid., 25.
5. Library of Congress Linked Data Service, Washington, DC, Library of Congress, 2009–, http://id.loc.gov.

6. *A Bibliographic Framework for the Digital Age* (Washington, DC: Library of Congress, October 31, 2011), www.loc.gov/bibframe/news/framework-103111.html; *Transforming Our Bibliographic Framework: A Statement from the Library of Congress* (Washington, DC: Library of Congress, May 13, 2011), www.loc.gov/bibframe/news/framework-051311.html.

7. Library of Congress Linked Data Service.

8. *MADS/RDF Primer* (Washington, DC: Library of Congress, 2013), www.loc.gov/standards/mads/rdf/.

9. "SKOS: Simple Knowledge Organization System Reference," W3C, 2009, www.w3.org/TR/2009/REC-skos-reference-20090818/.

10. "MARC Standards," Washington, DC, Network Development and MARC Standards Office, Library of Congress. www.loc.gov/marc/.

11. "Information and Documentation—Format for Information Exchange," Geneva, ISO, ISO 2709:2008.

12. "MARCXML: MARC 21 XML Schema," Washington, DC, Library of Congress, www.loc.gov/standards/marcxml/.

13. "Functional Requirements for Bibliographic Records," International Federation of Library Associations and Institutions, 1996, www.ifla.org/files/assets/cataloguing/frbr/frbr_2008.pdf; Godfrey Rust and Mark Bide, "The <indecs> Metadata Framework, Principles, Model and Data Dictionary," in Indecs, 2000, www.doi.org/topics/indecs/indecs_framework_2000.pdf; International Council of Museums, "CIDOC Conceptual Reference Model (CRM)" (ISO 21127:2014). www.cidoc-crm.org/index.html.

14. "Bibliographic Framework as a Web of Data: Linked Data Model and Supporting Services," Washington, DC, Library of Congress, November 21, 2012, www.loc.gov/bibframe/pdf/marcld-report-11–21–2012.pdf.

15. Bibliographic Framework Transition Initiative Forum, http://listserv.loc.gov/archives/bibframe.html.

16. GitHub, https://github.com.

17. "BIBFRAME AV Modeling Study: Defining a Flexible Model for Description of Audiovisual Resources," Washington, DC, Library of Congress, 2014, www.loc.gov/bibframe/pdf/bibframe-avmodelingstudy-may15–2014.pdf.

ABOUT THE CONTRIBUTORS

CAROL JEAN GODBY has directed projects with a focus on automated content analysis that produce research prototypes, open source software, improvements to national and international standards, and enhancements to OCLC's products, services, and data architecture. She has a Ph.D. in linguistics from Ohio State University. Since 2012 she has been the leader of a cross-division team at OCLC whose charter is to develop a next-generation data architecture based on the principles of linked data.

IKER HUERGA received his M.Sc. degree in computer science and electrical engineering from the University of Mondragon, Spain. He has been working on Semantic Web technologies applied to the health care and life sciences domain since early 2005, as a member of the Advisory Committee to the World Wide Web Consortium (W3C) from 2008 to 2009, and of the Health Care and Life Sciences Interest Group (HCLSIG) at W3C since 2008. Huerga started his career in academia, and soon went on to found two health care startups. He worked for three years at Elsevier Inc., as a lead Semantic Web engineer, and is currently the lead data science architect at the Memorial Sloan Kettering Cancer Center in New York City. His work has been published in *Pharmacogenomics* and the *International Journal of Metadata, Semantics and Ontologies*, among others.

ED JONES is associate director for library assessment and technical services at National University in San Diego. He is the author of *RDA and Serials Cataloging* (2013) and various journal articles, book chapters, and technical reports. He has spoken on library linked data at professional conferences and deals with it as a member of the Standing Committee on Standards of the Program for Cooperative Cataloging. He has held positions at Youngstown

State University, followed by the University of Michigan and Harvard. In 1994 he received his doctorate from the University of Illinois at Urbana-Champaign, followed by a few years teaching. In 1997 he moved to San Diego, where he worked initially for Information Quest, a journal metadata aggregator, before taking his current position.

MIKE LAURUHN is a librarian and currently disruptive technology director at Elsevier Labs. His research areas include linked data, library linked data, and datasets and their applications within scholarly and research communications. His current projects are in the governance, promotion, and integration of open vocabularies and other resources so that they can be used to enable more precise curation and annotation of research data and scientific communication.

SALLY H. McCALLUM is chief of the Network Development and MARC Standards Office at the Library of Congress. Her office has spearheaded the development of the Bibliographic Framework Initiative (BIBFRAME), and is also engaged in XML representations of widely used bibliographic formats, including MARCXML, MODS, and MADS, and development work with RDF. In addition to maintaining the MARC 21 formats, her office maintains other key library standards such as the information retrieval protocols Z39.50 and SRU, and PREMIS, the standard for preservation metadata for digital objects. Her office also develops services that can be used to explore the marriage of bibliographic description and the Web, such as the LC Linked Data Service (ID.loc.gov) and the BIBFRAME conversions and editor. McCallum has participated in a number of standards-related activities through the National Information Standards Organization (NISO), the International Standards Organization (ISO), and the International Federation of Library Associations and Institutions (IFLA). She has chaired and served on various boards and subcommittees of these organizations. She has published a number of articles on standards and networking. McCallum has a BA from Rice University and an MLS from the University of Chicago, with study in literature, mathematics, and information science.

ALLISON JAI O'DELL is metadata librarian and associate university librarian at the University of Florida, George A. Smathers Libraries. She is a coeditor for the ARLIS/NA *Artists' Books Thesaurus* and the RBMS *Controlled Vocabularies for Use in Rare Book and Special Collections Cataloging*, two library thesauri which are being published as linked open data.

M. CRISTINA PATTUELLI is an associate professor at the School of Information and Library Science at Pratt Institute, New York, where she teaches courses on knowledge organization, cultural heritage, and art documentation. Her current research explores the intersection between cultural heritage and information access, description, and design. She is the director of the Linked Jazz Project, which investigates the application of linked open data technology to cultural heritage resources.

MICHELE SEIKEL is a tenured professor on the library faculty at Oklahoma State University. She has held positions at Norman Public Library, the University of Oklahoma, and Stanford University, and served as a professional librarian at Oklahoma Panhandle State University and at Oklahoma State University. Seikel's primary professional focus is in cataloging, and she has published several research papers in technical services journals. In the ALA, she has cochaired the Cataloging Norms Interest Group and the Cataloging and Metadata Management Section's Policy and Planning Committee. Currently, she chairs the ALCTS Planning Committee, and is a member of the editorial board of the journal *Library Resources and Technical Services.*

CARL G. STAHMER, PhD, is the director of digital scholarship at the University Library, University of California, Davis, in which capacity he oversees a variety of digital initiatives on campus. Stahmer has been working in the field of digital humanities since the mid-1990s, when he began constructing the Romantic Circles website (www.rc.umd.edu), named then by the National Endowment for the Humanities as one of the top twenty educational websites in the world. In addition to creating and maintaining a host of academic websites, Stahmer has also worked as a computer programmer and system architect for a variety of governmental, academic, and commercial technology initiatives over the past twenty years. He has served as the associate director of the Maryland Institute for Technology and the Humanities at the University of Maryland, as a member of the Advisory Board of the Networked Infrastructure for Nineteenth-Century Studies, and as director of technology for Lynchinteractive Inc., where he was lead developer and system architect for a variety of Internet-based, advanced data-integration solutions, including medical, distance learning, and government information systems.

HILARY K. THORSEN is currently metadata librarian for humanities at Stanford University Libraries. She holds an MS in library and information science from Pratt Institute and an MA in photography history and criticism from Sotheby's Institute of Art, London. As a graduate student, she served as project manager for the Linked Jazz project and now she serves as a consultant.

INDEX

Lightning Source UK Ltd.
Milton Keynes UK
UKOW05f2134300916

284164UK00003B/223/P